THE SHIELD
OF PERSEUS

The Vision and Imagination
of Howard Nemerov

by

Julia A. Bartholomay

UNIVERSITY OF FLORIDA PRESS
GAINESVILLE 1972

Library of Congress Cataloging in Publication Data
Bartholomay, Julia A   1923–
     The shield of Perseus.

     Bibliography: p.
     1.   Nemerov, Howard.   I.   Title.
PS3527.E5Z58   811'.5'4   70–137851
ISBN 0–8130–0317–2

A University of Florida Press Book

*Poems quoted partially or in full
by permission of Howard Nemerov*

For Ann Louise Hentz
my teacher and friend who has shared this adventure
from its beginning, with
gratitude and affection.

CONTENTS

v

ABBREVIATIONS

POETRY

IL   *The Image and the Law*. New York: Henry Holt, 1947.

GR   *Guide to the Ruins*. New York: Random House, 1950.

SG   *The Salt Garden*. Boston: Little, Brown and Co., 1955.

MW   *Mirrors & Windows: Poems*. Chicago: University of Chicago Press, 1958.

NSP   *New & Selected Poems*. Chicago: University of Chicago Press, 1960.

NRD   *The Next Room of the Dream*. Chicago: University of Chicago Press, 1962.

BS   *The Blue Swallows*. Chicago: University of Chicago Press, 1967.

PROSE*

PF   *Poetry and Fiction: Essays*. New Brunswick, N.J.: Rutgers University Press, 1963.

Journal   *Journal of the Fictive Life*. New Brunswick, N.J.: Rutgers University Press, 1965.

*Page numbers occur in parentheses in text.

INTRODUCTION

Dᴜʀɪɴɢ ᴛʜᴇ ᴘᴀsᴛ twenty years, while literary styles shifted as fast as the hemline, Howard Nemerov has quietly, with stubborn integrity, gone about his business, teaching and writing. Today he is regarded by an increasing number of critics and readers as one of the major poets writing in English, as well as an accomplished novelist and critic. He has published, to date, seven books of poetry: *The Image and the Law, Guide to the Ruins, The Salt Garden, Mirrors & Windows: Poems, New & Selected Poems, The Next Room of the Dream,* and *The Blue Swallows.* In addition, he has produced two plays in verse, two collections of short stories, three novels, and the autobiographical *Journal of the Fictive Life.* As critic and lecturer, he has published numerous essays and speeches, many of which are collected in his *Poetry and Fiction: Essays* and *Reflexions on Poetry and Poetics.* For several years he worked on the magazine *Furioso.* He has edited *Poets in Progress* (to which he contributed an essay) and a book of Longfellow's poems (with introduction) for the Laurel Poetry Series.

Nemerov, as a man and a poet, eludes standard classifications. A self-styled "Jewish Puritan of the middle class" (*Journal,* 20) and a "square," he has a predilection for

1

wry epithets and epigrams which often belie his complex and deeply divided nature. He was born in New York City on March 1, 1920, of wealthy and cultivated parents. *Journal of the Fictive Life* recalls a sensitive, imaginative, and introverted little boy who "was most frequently criticized by . . . mother for being shy, sullen, uncommunicative" (19). Educated in private institutions, he graduated from the Fieldston Preparatory School in 1937 with a distinguished record as a student and athlete. The following year he went to Harvard College, where he began to write poetry, which, he says, "was the fashionable thing to do." Regarding his early efforts in versifying, he writes: "My roommate, who wrote a prize poem in freshman year, looked over my shoulder at my first attempts: 'Don't you know it's supposed to scan?' he said. I didn't. He has since become a novelist. (Maybe that's why my poems sometimes scan, even in a time where many poets try desperately not to.)"[1] In his junior year Nemerov won the Bowdoin Prize for an essay on Thomas Mann. (Mann and Kenneth Burke are the two fathers "in the spirit" referred to in connection with the first dream in *Journal of the Fictive Life*.) After his graduation in June 1941, Nemerov joined the RAF Coastal Command as an aviator and was based in England, where he later served with the Eighth United States Army Air Force. In 1944 he married an English girl and, following his discharge as a first lieutenant in 1945, they came to New York City to live.

After the war "two roads diverged" for Nemerov and he "chose the one less travelled by." He became a poet against the will of his father, who wanted him to enter the family business. For an only son to make such a decision was hard and not without lasting pain and guilt, as the *Journal* records: "As well as having its religiously exalted mystique, writing was for me at the beginning sinful and a transgression. That is to say, the emphasis I place to this

1. Personal letter, October 18, 1970.

day on work . . . contains a guilty acknowledgement that I became a writer very much against the will of my father, who wanted me to go into his business, or, as it used to be called, go to *work*" (13). This inward separation, a dominant theme in the *Journal*, is reconciled in all aspects as the book ends, very beautifully, with the birth of the Nemerovs' second son.

For Nemerov, as for most young poets, writing was a greater source of pleasure than income. After a year (during which the *Image and the Law* was written), he taught at Hamilton College and, in 1948, joined the English Department of Bennington College in Vermont, with which he was affiliated until 1966 when he went to Brandeis University in Massachusetts. Interim teaching appointments included a year as visiting lecturer in English at the University of Minnesota (1958–1959) and a year as writer-in-residence at Hollins College in Virginia (1962–1963). In 1969 he left Brandeis to become the Hurst Professor of Literature (1969–1970) at Washington University, where he is currently a Professor of English.

During the past fifteen years Nemerov's audience has grown appreciably, and the highest public recognition has been accorded him. He received the 1963–1964 appointment as consultant to the Library of Congress. In 1965 he was elected to membership in the National Institute of Arts and Letters; and in 1966 he was made a fellow of the American Academy of Arts and Sciences. Among his numerous awards are a Guggenheim Fellowship (1968), the first Theodore Roethke Memorial Award, given in 1968 for *The Blue Swallows,* and the 1971 Frank O'Hara Prize (offered for the fifth time by the Frank O'Hara Foundation for Poetry and Art) for his poems in the December 1970 issue of *Poetry*. Having received the 1971 Annual Fellowship of the Academy of American Poets, Nemerov is now an Honorary Fellow of the Academy.

Nemerov's work reveals his many-faceted intellect and

informed understanding of the arts, science, religion, and philosophy. As Peter Meinke states, "the quality that sets Nemerov's writings apart from other modern writers is its consistent intelligence, a breadth of wit in the eighteenth-century sense of the word expanded to cover a very modern awareness of contemporary man's alienation and fragmentation."[2] A scholar, Nemerov is erudite without being pedantic. His poems and essays, ranging in theme from the topical to the abstruse, display a highly original intelligence which turns reflexively on its subject and develops new insights and patterns of meaning. Whether discussing "The Marriage of Theseus and Hippolyta" (*PF*, 17–24) or commenting on the banalities of contemporary life (e.g., "Life Cycle of Common Man," *NSP*, 16), Nemerov's voice and perspective are distinctly his own. Though strongly disciplined in his craft, his approach to experience is one of "attentiveness and obedience."[3] Because he continually views the world with a morning freshness, he is often likened to Thoreau, yet such a comparison seems rather specious in that Nemerov, unlike Thoreau, is not strictly a nature poet or a philosopher of nature. Both men perceive the visible world with the objectivity of naturalists and, as poets, draw analogies from natural forms. Both men regard the generative cycle as the supreme model of the artistic process but not for the same reasons. As a student and philosopher of nature, Thoreau discovers an animating principle manifested therein and expounds it as a way of life, whereas Nemerov probes more deeply into the problem of mind and world and finds the natural process ultimately secret and mysterious. Like Robert Frost, he begins and ends with the riddle of eternity.

Representing no poetic school or movement, Nemerov stands apart in his generation—a giant, if a lonely one, who continues to shun identification with literary fads and band-

2. *Howard Nemerov*, p. 6.
3. Nemerov, "Attentiveness and Obedience," p. 248.

wagons. Although Louise Bogan cited his work as "an example of the well-written intelligently ordered poetry that has been termed 'academic' by the experimentalists"[4] (and called "mandarin" by Kenneth Rexroth),[5] Nemerov has not engaged in the cold war between the "New England Poets" (academicians) and the "Black Mountain/Beat Group," representing the short-lived San Francisco Renaissance and the confessional poetry of the fifties and sixties. At a time when Whitman is very much in vogue, Nemerov speaks out for Frost as the dean of American poets. Currently, Nemerov appears to be moving in the direction of Frost in his later years—toward a simpler, more immediate, and epigrammatic form of expression.

As T. S. Eliot observed, "no poet, no artist of any art, has his complete meaning alone."[6] Having evolved from the continuum of Yeats, Eliot, Auden, and Stevens, Nemerov acknowledges their influence on his early work. However, in *The Salt Garden* these influences are mastered and a unique style emerges, which has continued to develop. Endowed with a brilliant mind, a kaleidoscopic eye, a sensitive ear, and a marvelous wit, Nemerov was born a poet. Such gifts combined with curiosity and awareness, a deep sense of calling, and an honest acceptance of the demands of his art, have made the poet's rise to eminence as inevitable as it is unspectacular.

One of the most intriguing questions is why, when they have been so well received, have Nemerov's poems remained largely unexplored. A perceptive, analytical resume of Nemerov, as poet and novelist, by Peter Meinke, published in 1968, marks the first attempt of a poet or critic to study his work as a whole. The poems have been widely reviewed, not always favorably; and his last four books have been lauded by his peers. Thom Gunn, reviewing *New*

4. "Books, Verse," p. 129.
5. "A Stranger on Madison Avenue."
6. "The Sacred Wood," p. 15.

& *Selected Poems*, states that one must "class him outside the category of a mere generation; for the book makes it clear that he is one of the best poets writing in English."[7] In *Babel to Byzantium* James Dickey devotes several pages to explaining why Nemerov's "poetic intelligence," wit, and other talents make him an outstanding poet in our time.[8] Yet, as Nemerov wrote to me: "for good or ill nobody seems to have much to say *about* what I write. They either dislike it rather harshly, or say it's underrated and very fine . . . but that's about it. Maybe it don't puzzle them enough?"[9] With the exception of Mr. Meinke's pamphlet, an essay by Robert D. Harvey ("A Prophet Armed: An Introduction to Howard Nemerov"), and Kenneth Burke's comprehensive explication of "The Scales of the Eyes," Nemerov's comment holds true. The question is why?

One oversimplified answer may be that he has never been "the man of the hour." With the aid of Madison Avenue and our sensation-seeking press, poets may either create their own legends in life or wait for death to apotheosize them. Nemerov's respect for the Muse, as well as his innate modesty and honesty, prohibits histrionics such as the dadaesque shock techniques of some of his contemporaries. Consequently, his reputation has grown slowly and without fanfare. Then, too, he has no interest in literary cults with their attendant disciples.

Another and perhaps more significant answer may be that Nemerov demands more from his readers than do most poets. He brings to his art an extensive knowledge of diverse areas of experience, and his imagery is, paradoxically, simple and complex, though never obscure. Like Blake and Coleridge, he presents images with objectivity, which is not to say that they are literal or not transformed into something rich and strange. However, he is never a solipsist —not even in the highly personal, surrealistic "The Scales of

7. "Outside Faction."
8. Pages 35–41.
9. Personal letter, June 23, 1968.

the Eyes." Just as we know that Blake's magnificent tiger
—with all of its terrible fascination—will never turn into
melted butter, so do we recognize that Nemerov's swallows
are real birds, whose being is not dependent on the poet's
consciousness or (as in the case of some poets) a lack of it.
Images, though used in an original way, are never distor-
tions. The mirror held up to nature may not always be
beautiful, but it is never cracked. In the *Journal* the poet
speaks to this point: "I also think of poetry as a matter of
listening for what the landscape says to you, a marvelous
duplication of the scene in syllables which 'happen to be'
appropriate. A certain simplicity is also requisite, even a
naivete; my example for this was that a poet who, seeing a
rock in the road, said, 'There is a rock in the road,' is a
real poet; the false poet would hoke it up in the transcrip-
tion" (173–74). Thus, the real poet does not confer his
own reality upon the world, playing the old game of twenty
questions—Who am I? Nemerov respects the facts that an
image is primarily a denotation of "some thing," before it
can be transformed, and that the language of poetry is a
relationship between the form and substance of things.

In spite of this apparent simplicity, Nemerov is exceedingly complex. His images are multivalent, governed by a
prismatic mind and eye, and have plural significance for
which the reader must dig. Nemerov's response to the
totality of experience presupposes a certain awareness on
the part of the reader, since the poet has a meaning to
convey through language, not through guesswork. For
example, the reader who has scientific understanding will
discover the organic beauty of the seed and water imagery
in "Runes" and experience the poem on all levels of meaning, whereas the reader who is not scientifically oriented
will regard the seed and water as symbols only, and will
miss the generative power of the poem.

For the reader who is willing to reach and respond to
Nemerov, there are great rewards. At the same time, his
work will be less interesting, as well as too difficult, for

those who want fun and games or the chance to play psycho-analyst. Unfortunately, relativism is the trend of the times, but if poetry is to have any lasting meaning, it must go beyond the relative and be judged accordingly. Cleanth Brooks has already warned us against seeing a poem merely as an expression of its age as if "any attempt to view it *sub specie aeternitatis* . . . must result in illusion." He also warns that poetry so reduced "becomes significant merely as cultural anthropology and the poetry of the present, merely as a political, or religious, or moral instrument." Yet, as he says, "the miracle of communication remains."[10] With Nemerov one experiences that miracle, for "writing is in some sense speaking to someone, it is also an act of love, or faith; that something is able to be said, that someone will listen . . ." (*Journal*, 58).

As one who has listened, I believe that the vision and the unique talent of Howard Nemerov will be revealed through a study of his complex imagery, too long unexplored. In the preparation of this book, I have been grateful for Peter Meinke's fine pamphlet (which I hope will be expanded to a book) and for his concise resume of the salient facts of Nemerov's life, which I have followed closely in this introduction. As would be expected, Mr. Meinke and I, along with several others, have often come to the same conclusions. We have recognized Nemerov's "double vision," his use of tragicomic paradox, his use of light imagery, and his "philosophy of minimal affirmation" —in Mr. Meinke's words. I acknowledge also my debt to Robert D. Harvey for his helpful analysis of the poem "The Salt Garden" and to Kenneth Burke for his perceptive explication of "The Scales of the Eyes." Burke's observations provide valuable clues to Nemerov's method and work as a whole, as well as to an understanding of this complex poem sequence.

The ultimate value in writing this book is to dis-

10. *The Well-Wrought Urn*, pp. x, xi.

cover just what *is* a good poem. The ultimate risk is to render the poetry as it is not, or to read oneself into the poems. On the last point, I am reassured by the poet's words. "When I say over these things, I say them as myself and not myself, as a possibility of certain grandeurs and contempts in the self which the poet alone has been able to release, and I ask whether the voice that speaks at this moment is more his or mine, or whether poetry is not in this respect the most satisfactory of many unsatisfactory ways we have of expressing our sense that we are members of one another. That voice, which I add by reading, or which the poet adds to me when I read, a voice which in some ways belongs to neither of us personally, is a third voice of poetry. . . . And there is still one further voice of poetry to be considered. . . . That is the voice of an eternally other, the resonance that in our repetition of the poet's words seems to come from outside where 'the shadow of an external world draws near.' "[11]

11. "The Bread of Faithful Speech," in *PF*, pp. 91–92.

1

A DOCTRINE OF SIGNATURES

In a recent poem, Howard Nemerov describes the artist as one who "sees / How things must be continuous with themselves / As with whole worlds that they themselves are not, / In order that they may be so transformed."[1] These words also transcribe the poetic intelligence and imagination which inform Nemerov's poems. His lens is prismatic, and his ear is attuned to fresh articulating possibilities in all areas of being. He sees paradox in all phenomena and how the most unlike things define each other and, in so doing, gain their identity. Therefore, his imagination, moving on many levels of experience, is paradoxical, reflexive, and generative. It mirrors the dynamic tensions and continuity between the one and the other which, in the course of their becoming, are transformed through language. For a moment in eternity, that which is spatial and temporal becomes actual in the poem. This capacity of the mind, limited though it is, to perceive, imagine, and articulate the invisible, is clarified best by the poet:

Language, then, is the marvelous mirror of the human condition, a mirror so miraculous that it can see what

1. *The Painter Dreaming in the Scholar's House*, p. 3.

is invisible, that is, the relations between things. At the same time, the mirror is a limit, and as such, it is sorrowful; one wants to break it and look beyond. But unless we have the singular talent for mystical experience we do not really break the mirror, and even the mystic's experience is available to us only as reflected, inadequately, in the mirror. Most often man deals with reality by its reflection. That is the sense of Perseus' victory over the Gorgon by consenting to see her only in the mirror of his shield, and it is the sense of the saying in Corinthians that we see now as through a glass darkly—a phrase rendered by modern translators as "now we see as in a little mirror" ("The Swaying Form," in *PF*, 11–12).

To discover Nemerov's vision, as it is articulated in the mirror of language, requires some understanding of his purpose and method, for poems, whatever their ultimate concern, are produced by human beings and are functional —not in a pejorative way but in the sense of Marianne Moore's adjective "useful." As Nemerov and other thinkers have noted, much of modern poetry tends to have a single reflexive dimension pertaining to the process of composition itself. In fact, this development of the mind curving back upon itself may always be a limit for every kind of thought. Shakespeare observed, without considering it strange at all, that "speculation turns not to itself / Till it hath travell'd, and is mirror'd there / Where it may see itself."[2] But in the world today—"that palace of mirrors where, says Valery, the lonely lamp is multiplied"[3]—man feels estranged. As Nemerov suggests, the problem of identity may underlie the fact that so much reflexive poetry is being written and that so many poets have sought to

2. "The Swaying Form," in *PF*, p. 9. Nemerov quotes Shakespeare, *Troilus and Cressida*, 3.3.109–11. (Although "married," not "mirror'd," is now accepted by most modern editors; see Shakespeare, *Troilus and Cressida*, New Variorum Edition, p. 177.)
3. Ibid.

analyze and define the creative process and the poem. Since the poet refers to himself, as well as to his contemporaries, the study of his work may properly begin with his concept of poetry and the creative process, his belief in imagination as the agent of reality, and his use of reflexive imagery to express, in the mirror of language, the invisible relation between mind and world.

With Nemerov, as with all true poets, the vision and its articulation are one in intention, inasmuch as poems define themselves through their own creation. As the poet writes in a letter, referring to Richards, Empson, and Burke, "These men see how in some sense, not invariably a visible sense, words always have to be about themselves, hence how poems, whatever they say they're about, are also talking about their own coming into being."[4] Recognizing the problem of definition, Nemerov has, nevertheless, meditated deeply on the question of "what is a poem"—in numerous essays, in *Journal of the Fictive Life,* and throughout his seven books of poetry. Characteristically, such inquiry has produced no pat answer nor aesthetic theory about art and life, but rather a series of reflections on a theme—a continuous redefinition of poetry as a way of being:

> one way of doing
> One's being in a world
> Whose being is both thought
> And thing, where neither thing
> Nor thought will do alone
> Till either answers other;
> Two lovers in the night
> Each sighing other's name
> Whose alien syllables
> Become synonymous
> For all their mortal night

4. Personal letter, October 30, 1968.

And their embodied day:
    Fire in the diamond,
    Diamond in the dark.

    ("One Way," in *BS*, 86)

Another way of saying this: "poems are arrangements of language which illuminate a connection between the inside and the outside of things."[5] This thought, like the mirror concept, points to the source of poetry, the "great primary human drama," or, as Shakespeare says, echoing Dante, "all the story of the night told over."[6] Nemerov describes human drama as being all that mankind does and suffers in this world, the dark source to which the poet must always return: "Lyric poetry, just because of its great refinement, its subtlety, its power of immense implication in a confined space—a great reckoning in a little room—is perpetually in danger of preferring gesture to substance. It thins out, it goes through the motions, it shows no responsibility. I conceive this responsibility of poetry to be to great primary human drama, which poets tend to lose sight of because of their privilege of taking close-ups of single moments on the rim of the wheel of the human story" (*Journal*, 21).

The Muse, then, is chiefly concerned with life and death —with the self in all of the many worlds in which it lives and dies each day.[7] A jealous Muse, she demands all of the poet's devotion, integrity, and dedication to his art. He must name a situation, as honestly and accurately as possible, but always a situation which he himself is in. The name he applies must be so close a fit with the actuality evoked that no room remains between "inside and outside"; as Dante said, the thought must be "like a beast moving in its

5. Nemerov, "Younger Poets: The Lyric Difficulty," in *PF*, p. 224.
6. Nemerov, "The Marriage of Theseus and Hippolyta," in *PF*, p. 22 (Shakespeare, *A Midsummer Night's Dream*, 5.1.23).
7. Nemerov, "The Muse's Interest," in *PF*, p. 47.

skin."[8] This involves participation of the conscious/unconscious and of mind/body in reference to nature and the nature of things. The process is reflexive and cyclical—"a matter of feedback between oneself and 'it,' an 'it' which can gain identity only in the course of being brought into being, come into being only in the course of finding its identity."[9]

The means of becoming related to the nature of things is the "swaying form," suggested to the poet by Florio's translation of Montaigne: "There is no man (if he listen to himselfe) that doth not discover in himselfe a peculiar forme of his, a swaying forme, which wrestleth against the art and the institution, and against the tempest of passions, which are contrary to him."[10] Nemerov adds that this form is "simultaneously ruling and variable, or fickle; shifting and protean as the form of water in a stream," and can be identified with the libido, or impulse to art. Because this form escapes definition, refusing ever to become fixed, it corresponds to the poet's vision, which likewise can be described only according to its characteristics. As the poet tells us, " 'this vision' need not be thought of in religious terms, as a dramatic one-shot on the road to Damascus; its articulation may be slow indeed, and spread over many works; the early and late parts of it may elucidate one another, or encipher one another still more deeply." Because "the vision *is* itself alone," without verbal equivalent, it is untranslatable to the rational understanding. The poet adds that a "fine description is given by Antony, the vision being disguised as a crocodile:

It is shaped, sir, like itself; and it is as broad as it hath breadth. It is just as high as it is, and moves with its own organs. It lives by that which nourisheth it; and the elements once out of it, it transmigrates . . .

8. Nemerov, "The Swaying Form," in *PF*, p. 13.
9. Ibid., p. 14.
10. Ibid., p. 6. (The phrase about "the art" is not included in all editions, according to Nemerov's footnote on page 6.)

&c., ending with the information that it is a strange serpent, and the tears of it are wet."[11]

Vision is the life substance of a poem: "for poetry exists only by a continuing revelation in a world always incarnate of word and flesh indissolubly, a world simultaneously solid and transpicuous. . . . Poetry and institutionalized religion are in a sense the flowing and the static forms of the same substance, liquid and solid states of the same elemental energy."[12] For this reason the poet and the prophet have always borne close association. Without meaning to (and perhaps without especially wanting to), poetry changes the mind of the world.[13]

The revelation (or "opening of the ways") occurs wherever a poet illuminates our human consciousness, or our sense of what it means to be human.[14] Communication is not effected by a universal truth or a moral value implied in the poem, but rather through the voice of the poet and his way of speaking. As he tells us again the story of the night, a transfiguration happens—in the poet's mind, in the mind of his audience, and, finally, in the minds of all who have ever retold the story. The tale thus "grows to something of great constancy" and harmony so that it "constitutes on its own a world of ordered relation, rhythm, and figure."[15] The poet, responding to primary human drama, brings forth numerous parables which his audience is responsible for interpreting. Such parables may contradict but they never exclude each other.

The difference, then, between poetry (or art) and life is a formal one. As Nemerov defines it, "Civilization, mirrored in language, is the garden where relations grow; outside the garden is the wild abyss. Poetry . . . is the art of contemplating this situation in the mirror of language."[16]

11. "The Muse's Interest," in *PF*, p. 45.
12. Nemerov, "The Swaying Form," in *PF*, p. 13.
13. Nemerov, "The Muse's Interest," in *PF*, p. 46.
14. Ibid.
15. Nemerov, "The Marriage of Theseus and Hippolyta," in *PF*, p. 23.
16. "The Swaying Form," in *PF*, p. 12.

The poet recalls that a philosopher of language once said that "see" and "say" derive from the same root, for "to say" is to make someone else "see" what you have seen.[17] In this sense, to name a situation is to illuminate again what has been there since the beginning of time, or since the beginning of the Word. Said another way, the poetic art is an intimate relationship between the visible and invisible—a continuous dialogue between form and substance and between the light and the darkness. Poetry endures where systems of religion, philosophy, and law fail, because it perpetually redefines itself, always reaching its beginning again.[18] "For the whole business of poetry is vision and the substance of this vision is the articulating possibilities still unknown, the concentrating what is diffuse, the bringing forth what is in darkness."[19]

Poetry has its secret beginnings in the garden, before the first moment of recognition that we know "that we know" and, therefore, are naked, divided, doubtful, and afraid before the Mystery. Aware of the darkness beyond the paradoxical mirror image, Nemerov writes in the *Journal*: "perhaps it was looking at that likeness of myself, seeing myself as a stranger, a mystery, that represented the secret beginnings of art, that mystery which brings me now to search the self in a spirit of guilt and isolation and some secrecy. Or else there is some meaningful episode belonging to the portrait, which I am unable to bring back because it represents something I can't look at" (75).

From first awareness of self, which is primarily sexual and religious in its concern about life and death, the poet grows to awareness of the physical world, which is primarily philosophical in its everlasting WHY?. The vast and complex vision of nature and its processes is reflexive

17. "Attentiveness and Obedience," p. 242.
18. Nemerov, "Younger Poets: The Lyric Difficulty," in *PF*, p. 224.
19. Nemerov, "The Muse's Interest," in *PF*, p. 46.

with the image of self; both are paradoxical, changing, and both involve the notion of living and dying, simultaneously, or of being and becoming. This generative relation between self and world is the creative process in art, described in the following excerpt from the *Journal* in which the poet recalls a "passage from Valery when he talks about Nature's always constructing her solid forms out of liquids," and adds: "It seems as though I have been saying, in a confused and 'historical' way, that art is the secret (holy, forbidden) observation of this process and its reverse, having to do with metamorphosis and the relation, or identity, of the evanescent with the enduring; that the model for this process is sexual and generative, so that one approaches it always with equal fascination and fear, as Milton approached the Spirit that 'from the first / Wast present, and with mighty wings outspread / Dove-like satst brooding on the vast Abyss / And madst it pregnant . . .' in a passage that began with Man's first disobedience, and the fruit of that forbidden tree, &c." (147). This fascination with the Mystery of Creation is fundamental to Nemerov's work, and the generative model is frequently ritualized in his poems as well as in the poetic process. The garden remains an infinite parable suggesting the articulating possibilities and limits of poetry as Nemerov imagines them; beyond the garden is the vast abyss. Out of this situation the poet's vision evolves, for, like all true poets, he is ultimately concerned with the mystery of being, that is, with creation and its reverse process—metamorphosis and the relation, or identity, of the evanescent with the enduring.

The substance of the vision, born out of darkness, is brought to light through the mind's eye, or imagination. In one sense, the imaginative process is limited, for what the mind invents, it also discovers. The less murky our glass becomes, the more we are stricken in the light of what we see—our own image bared in that of the Other. This dual

aspect of envisioning is a constant theme in Joseph Conrad's
work, to which Nemerov refers directly in "Runes," XIII
(*NSP*):

> . . . The sailor leaned
> To lick the mirror clean, the somber and
> Immense mirror that Conrad saw, and saw
> The other self, the sacred Cain of blood
> Who would seed a commonwealth in the Land of Nod.

Here is the limit of mind imagining. In his own way, Nemerov affirms the meaning of T. S. Eliot's statement that
"human kind cannot bear very much reality." Truth, as it is
revealed to us, is necessarily reflected and limited by imagination which is not only a mirror but also a shield to pro-
tect us from the blinding light of reality and to cover our
own nakedness and vulnerability. Without this shield, man
is stricken when he comes face to face with the Gorgon, as
Nemerov tells us, speaking in his own voice as "A Predecessor of Perseus":

> . . . But he rides his road
> Passing the skinless elder skeletons
> Who smile, and maybe he will keep on going
> Until the grey unbearable she of the world
> Shall raise her eyes and recognize, and grin
> At her eternal amateur's approach,
> All guts no glass, to meet her gaze head on
> And be stricken in the likeness of himself
> At least if not of Keats and Alexander.
>
> (*NRD*, 16)

However, in another, more primordial sense, imagination is as unlimited as the sea in which infinite possibilities
of expression exist in the rhythm and song of the tide.
Poetry, after all, is an aural art which grew out of the song

and dance of religious ritual, patterned after the natural
cycle. In the last two lines of "Painting a Mountain Stream"
(*NSP*, 58), the poet says: "Steady the wrist, steady the
eye; / paint this rhythm, not this thing." Poetry was born
of the spoken, not the written, word—this Nemerov remembers. In discussing the marked changes that have gradually
appeared in his work, he cites his growing consciousness
of "nature as responsive to language or, to put it the other
way, of imagination as the agent of reality." He adds that
this is a "magical idea and not very much heard of these
days among poets—practically never among critics."[20] The
same thought is expressed in *Journal of the Fictive Life*:
"My imagination is dominantly aural, and poetry for me is
not primarily 'imagery' but a sequence of sounds which
with their meanings form the miraculous equivalent of
something existing in nature" (84*n*).

This aural communication with reality remains a
mystery to Nemerov, for "why should a phrase come to you
out of the ground and seem to be exactly right?" Yet, he
believes this mystery to be a poet's proper relation with the
nature of things, "a relation in which language, that accum-
ulated folly and wisdom in which the living and dead speak
simultaneously, is a full partner and not merely a stenogra-
pher."[21] This mysterious relation, or dialogue, with nature
is illustrated in the poem "A Spell before Winter," which is
about Vermont at the end of fall, "when the conventional
glory of the leaves is over and the tourists have gone home,
and the land not only reveals itself in its true colors but
also, in the figure of the poem, speaks."[22] The last verse of
the poem is quoted below:

Now I can see certain simplicities
In the darkening rust and tarnish of the time,

20. "Attentiveness and Obedience," p. 241.
21. Ibid.
22. Ibid.

And say over the certain simplicities,
The running water and the standing stone,
The yellow haze of the willow and the black
Smoke of the elm, the silver, silent light
Where suddenly, readying toward nightfall,
The sumac's candelabrum darkly flames.
And I speak to you now with the land's voice,
It is the cold, wild land that says to you
A knowledge glimmers in the sleep of things:
The old hills hunch before the north wind blows.

(*NRD*, 19)

This is a miniature tone poem in which mood and meaning are conveyed through sound and rhythm rather than through image, symbol, or metaphor. Visually, of course, these lines paint a landscape, an arrangement of contrasting colors and shapes, blended into a single impression. But thematic unity is created by aural rather than visual means—through the deft use of tone, stress, and cadence. The standard poetic musical devices (alliteration, assonance, internal rhyme, etc.) are used here with discretion, since the poet does not depend on them. Each syllable has the quantity and quality of a musical note; each phrase is a musical entity in relation to the whole tonal pattern. "A Spell before Winter" and "Painting a Mountain Stream," more than any of Nemerov's poems, combine the imaginative concept and process, displaying the purity and power of the poet's sensitive but disciplined ear.

Despite the simplicity of statement and grace of style in these lyrics (and in others like them), Nemerov's concept of imagination and his multivalent imagery are too complex to be defined in strictly aural terms. Imagination is both limited (visually) and unlimited (aurally), as has been noted. Perhaps this basic perceptual dualism underlies the two different, though not necessarily antithetical, attitudes which appear consistently in the poet's work. On the one hand, he is very much the witty, sophisticated, and urbane man of his time, particularly when he writes in the satirical vein. Aware of man's dehumanization in an automated mass society where the split human condition is intensified, Nemerov often views life with a humorous but bitter irony. When he spoofs society, the visual impact is strong; witness "Blue Suburban," "Mrs. Mandrill," "Boom!," "Keeping Informed in D.C.," or "Life Cycle of Common Man"[23]—the last lines of which are quoted below:

> Consider the courage in all that, and behold the man
> Walking into deep silence, with the ectoplastic
> Cartoon's balloon of speech proceeding
> Steadily out of the front of his face, the words
> Borne along on the breath which is his spirit
> Telling the numberless tale of his untold Word
> Which makes the world his apple, and forces him to eat.

> *(NSP,* 17)

On the other hand, the poet perceives the world ontologically. His experience may be philosophical, subjective, lyrical, or even mystical. In the poems where his vision moves outward or inward toward the Mystery, his imagination is dominantly aural. Poetry becomes a matter of listening to the landscape, and he envisions a world made intelligible through imagination, through language—spirit and word: ". . . I do not now, if I ever did, consent to the common modern view of language as a system of conventional signs for the passive reception of experience, but tend ever more to see language as making an unknowingly large part of a material world whose independent existence might be likened to that of the human unconscious, a sleep of causes, a chaos of the possible-impossible, responsive only to the

---

23. "Blue Suburban" is from *NRD,* p. 35; "Mrs. Mandrill" and "Boom!" are from *NSP,* pp. 20–21 and 18–19; and "Keeping Informed in D.C." is from *BS,* p. 62.

wakening touch of desire and fear—that is, to spirit; that is, to the word."[24]

The dual aspects of Nemerov, as a man and poet, are not unique in themselves, but what *is* original is the way in which his imagination reflects the vision that has evolved over the years through his poems. While there is no particular period when one or the other attitude dominates, a parallel does exist between the development of the man and that of the poet. His first three books, filled with wit, satire, irony, and ambiguity, are primarily the work of a young urban poet who writes of what he knows: the city, war, and the paradox between the ideal and actual—all fairly universal topics. The titles of these books read like a Baedecker of the postwar world: *Guide to the Ruins, The Image and the Law*, and *The Salt Garden*. However, even in these volumes, the identity of the poet is emerging in such poems as "Under the Bell Jar," "Lot's Wife," "Unscientific Postscript," and "The Scales of the Eyes."[25] The following lines suggest the unique vision and concept of imagination to come:

There is the world, the dream, and the one law.
The wish, the wisdom, and things as they are.

Inside the cave the burning sunlight showed
A shade and forms between the light and shade,

Neither real nor false nor subject to belief:
If unfleshed, boneless also, not for life

Or death or clear idea. But as in life
Reflexive, multiple, with the brilliance of

The shining surface, and orchestral flare. . . .

("Unscientific Postscript," in *IL*, 69)

24. "Attentiveness and Obedience," p. 241.
25. The first three poems mentioned are in *IL*; "The Scales of the Eyes" is in *SG*.

While originality in image and style are not quite reached in the early books, their tone is distinct and they contain a number of excellent poems. Aware of his imperfections, the poet comments: "Stylistically, I began under the aegis of notions drawn, I suppose, chiefly from T. S. Eliot. Along with many other beginners, I learned to value irony, difficulty, erudition, and the Metaphysical style of composition after the example of John Donne. . . . I now regard simplicity and the appearance of ease in the measure as primary values, and the detachment of a single thought from its ambiguous surrounding as a worthier object than the deliberate cultivation of ambiguity."[26] He adds that, "brought up to a poetry of irony, paradox, and wit as primary means of imagination," he cannot sharply divide the comic from the serious, or even from the sorrowful. However this penchant for humor has been honed over the years to a powerful talent, and it is in the tragicomic paradox that the two dominant strains of the poet's voice most frequently synchronize. As James Dickey writes, Nemerov is "one of the funniest, wittiest poets we have": "And it is true, too, that in his most serious poems there is an element of mocking, or self-mocking. But the enveloping emotion that arises . . . is helplessness; the helplessness we all feel in the face of the events of our time, and of life itself. . . . And beneath even this feeling is a sort of hopelessly involved acceptance and resignation which has in it far more of the truly tragic than most poetry which deliberately sets out in quest of tragedy."[27]

While irony, wit, and paradox, often expressed through punning, are still part of Nemerov's imaginative process, the years of apprenticeship were brief and, with the publication of *The Salt Garden* in 1955, it was apparent that the real poet had come into his own. In many of the poems in this volume, the city and the early guideposts recede, and

26. "Attentiveness and Obedience," p. 240.
27. *Babel to Byzantium*, p. 40.

the poet has found his sense of direction. Speaking to this point, Randall Jarrell remarks, "Behind the old poems there was a poet trying to write poetry; behind these new ones there is a man with interests and experiences of his own, that is, a poet who has learned to write poetry."[28]

Without consciously seeking his voice, Nemerov has found it. There is no doubt that the aural quality of his imagination responded to the beauty and simplicity of life in the natural environment in which he has lived for most of the past twenty-three years. Nevertheless, he is not a "nature poet" in the limited sense of that term; nor is he, like Frost, a philosopher of nature, although he is often philosophical in the parables he draws from there. What he searches for is the reality that binds us to the natural world in spite of our dusty myopic lenses, lost instincts, and pretty thoughts about it. Frequently he perceives nature with a scientific eye, looking for answers in the branching relation of trees in a snowfall, in a dried-up pond from which a dragonfly emerges, or in a maimed turtle that "takes a secret wound out of the world."[29] Often the correspondence between internal and external situation is conveyed through powerfully descriptive elemental imagery as, for example, in "Runes," "Brainstorm," "A Day on the Big Branch," and "The Quarry." Sometimes the poet's response is fanciful, as in "Holding the Mirror up to Nature" and "Celestial Globe." At other times nature is transfigured through the poet's private lens to express a particular mood, as in "The Sunglasses," "The Icehouse in Summer," and "The Sanctuary."[30] Always he respects nature's forms and substance and its mutability. What he seeks, as do all poets, is to

28. "Recent Poetry," p. 126.
29. "The View from an Attic Window" and "The Pond," in *NSP*, pp. 22–23 and 42–46; and "The Mud Turtle," in *BS*, pp. 97–98.
30. "The Quarry," "A Day on the Big Branch," "Brainstorm," "The Sanctuary" (all from earlier volumes), "Runes," and "The Icehouse in Summer" can be found in *NSP*; "The Sunglasses" and "Holding the Mirror up to Nature" are in *MW*; "Celestial Globe" is in *BS*.

find again that world of nature which Shakespeare imagined —a world that is at once sublime and terrible but is also a reality which no poet afterwards has regained.

The problem of imagination today is that of the post-Shakespearian world, or the modern age of poetry, and is a matter to which Nemerov has given considerable thought. To understand his imagery one must know the context of this problem. Currently, the imagination (once thought to be too real to argue about) is subject to a great deal of research in an attempt to "locate" and define "mind" in its spatial and temporal dimensions—another extension of man's search for identity. The relationship between mind and world (or even the possibility that such exists) is continually questioned, while man's self-image daily becomes more fragmented and absurd.

The mind's relation with the world is discussed by Nemerov in one of his most penetrating essays, "Two Ways of the Imagination." His premise is that, during the modern age, poetry "has had increasingly to define itself in relation to the conventional worldly view" concerning the relationship between soul and body, mind and world—the traditional subject of poetry.[31] The conventional view is what Alfred North Whitehead has termed "scientific materialism,": a "fixed cosmology which presupposes the ultimate fact of an irreducible brute matter, or material, spread throughout space in a flux of configurations. In itself such a material is senseless, valueless, purposeless."[32] What has resulted, Nemerov says, is the "so-called alienation of poetry from society," as a "function of this self-definition," and

31. "The Mind's Relation with the World," p. 375.
32. Ibid. Nemerov quotes Whitehead, *Science and the Modern World*, p. 25. "Matter," as Whitehead conceived of it, has been reduced, of course, so it can no longer be considered as "irreducible" in scientific terms. According to Whitehead, Einstein's theory that mass (or matter) and energy are equivalent to each other ($E = mc^2$) made it possible to show the conversion of matter into energy, and vice versa; nevertheless, the problem of where to locate mind remains, as a result of "scientific materialism."

also "an observable tendency for poetry to become the subject of itself."

Scientific abstractions, as Whitehead stated, have yielded matter on the one hand, "with its simple location in space and time," and "on the other hand 'mind,' perceiving, suffering, reasoning, but not interfering." Philosophy has been compelled to accept such abstractions as "the most concrete rendering of fact," which has produced three theories about the mind: dualism (mind and matter accepted on an equal basis) and two types of monism, one placing mind inside matter and the other, matter inside mind.

In view of this historical development in science and philosophy, the growing tendency of poetry to become its own subject and alienated from society is an attempt to solve the problem of mind/world by means of the imagination—an attempt which proceeds from doubt. Nemerov's thesis is that poems, through analogy upon analogy, seek to imagine their own imagining, or coming into being. Wordsworth, in "The Prelude," and Blake, in "Jerusalem," were the first great poets to write self-reflective poems, and these illustrate two ways of the imagination. Both poets introduced something new into poetry, which is "doubt." This "doubt" was what "led them to view their own vocations as problematic and subject to investigation." Nemerov believes that the element of doubt in no way diminishes the claims of the imagination but rather that the reverse is true. "Imagination now becomes central to the universe and the most important thing to understand about the universe; but becomes this precisely because it has become problematic and doubtful."[33]

These lines echo the inverse logic and paradoxical perspective of many modern philosophers and theologians who, likewise, see the impossibility of man ever perceiving the One except in terms of the Other. Here, also, is echoed the

33. Ibid., p. 378.

problem of language itself, particularly the language of poetry. Cleanth Brooks consistently makes the point that paradoxes spring from the nature of the poet's language: "it is a language in which the connotations play as great a part as the denotations."[34] Brooks adds that if "the poet is to be true to his poetry he must call it neither two nor one: the paradox is his only solution. The difficulty has intensified since Shakespeare's day: the timid poet, when confronted with the problem of 'Single Nature's double name,' has too often funked it."[35]

Far from being timid, Nemerov continually strives to solve the riddle of the Phoenix in his poems and in his reflections on the nature of language and the imaginative process. In the tradition of Richards, Empson, and Burke, he has even added a third dimension to the paradox in his poem "Phoenix," namely, the idea that words, besides being denotative and connotative, are also reflexive, being about themselves:

> The Phoenix comes of flame and dust
> He bundles up his sire in myrrh
> A solar and unholy lust
> Makes a cradle of his bier
>
> In the City of the Sun
> He dies and rises all divine
> There is never more than one
> Genuine
>
> By incest, murder, suicide
> Survives the sacred purple bird
> Himself his father, son and bride
> And his own Word.

(NSP, 116)

34. Cleanth Brooks, *The Well-Wrought Urn*, p. 8.
35. Ibid., p. 20.

Comparison of the poem with Shakespeare's "The Phoenix and the Turtle" shows the direction of the poetic imagination since the Renaissance. From his vantage point in space and time, Nemerov's lens is necessarily more divided than Shakespeare's, yet, in many ways, their vision is the same. With a little serendipity the reader discovers that what Nemerov writes about Shakespeare's world correlates with something in his own world of imagination:

> Shakespeare's tragedies seem to work on the belief, deep enough to require no justification, that there exist several distinct realms of being, which for all their apparent distinctiveness respond immediately and decisively to one another. . . . All these mutually reflect one another. You cannot disturb the balance of one mind, or of one king's court, without the seismic registration of that disturbance in the near and remotest regions of the cosmos: an error of judgment will strike flat the thick rotundity of the world; a wicked thought will tumble together the treasure of nature's germens even till destruction sicken. The result is a world of dreadful splendors, but every piece of it is rhythmically articulated with every piece; and the realms which have priority in initiating the great releases of energy are ambiguously psychological and supernatural at once, but unequivocally the realms of spirit, will, mind. All life, and all the scene of life, the not-living around and beneath and above, poise in a trembling balance which is complete, self-moving, extensive in detail through the four elements, from "Let Rome in Tiber melt" and "kingdoms are clay" to "I am fire and air" and "O eastern star!" This, then, is the sublime and terrible treasure which afterwards was lost. . . .[36]

Compare this vision of Shakespeare's with what Nemerov says in regard to the universe:

36. "The Mind's Relation with the World," pp. 376–77.

The painter Delacroix expressed it by saying that Nature is a dictionary. Everything is there, but not in the order one needs. The universe itself, so far as we relate ourselves to it by the mind, may be not so much a meaning as a rhythm, a continuous articulation of question and answer, a musical dialectic precipitating out moments of meaning which become distinct only as one wave does in a sea of waves ("The Swaying Form," in *PF*, 11).

The two visions of the universe are able to correspond, despite the difference in the poets' lenses, because of the bifocal nature of imagination. Mind appropriates and con-cretizes human experience within a historical context, yet the substance of all imagery, in any age, is elemental and, therefore, atemporal—even aspatial—however we may describe or interpret it. As Nemerov reminds us, all poets at some time come into relation with the "initiatory ascent from earth through water and air to fire"[37]—an ascent which may be gradual or cyclical. Similarly, poetry con-tinues to ritualize the natural pattern of birth, death, and regeneration, in both the poem and the poetic process. Because nature is the raw material of imagery in poetry, as in all art, and since the source of poetry is the primary human drama, the vision articulated through a particular work (or works) can transcend historical limitations as well as those of the art form itself. This happens in spite of, though also because of, the fact that imagination is dual. Through the substance of vision the unitive possibility exists for poets of widely different eras (and for artists working in different media)—a possibility which, paradoxi-cally, can *only* exist because of the particular nature and function of imagination moving within and through the limits of the art form. This dual function of imagination is implied in Nemerov's description of the painter as one who

37. Ibid., p. 384.

"sees / How things must be continuous with themselves /
As with whole worlds that they themselves are not, /
In order that they may be so transformed." The same implication can be found in the poet's statement about the poetic
process being "a matter of feedback between oneself and
'it,' an 'it' which can gain identity only in the course of
being brought into being, come into being only in the course
of finding its identity."

Specifically, the dual function of the poetic imagination
is to listen attentively, then, to transform what is heard
into a vision that is as organically sound and just as elusive
to the rational understanding as Antony's crocodile. The
means of transformation is art, which is not the least part
of the lyric difficulty, as Nemerov asserts. A poem must
illumine a connection between the visible and invisible. "The
durability of poems, as objects made out of language
which will be around for some time because people experience this illumination and therefore like reading them,
results from the clarity, force, and coherence with which
this connection is made, and not from anything else however laudable, like the holding of strong opinions, or the
feeling of strong emotions, or the naming of beautiful
objects."[38] As a means of transformation, art need not be
true to life or love (though both are involved); art must
be true only to the voice of imagination and to the rigid
demands of the art form itself. This point is illustrated by
an aphorism in the *Journal*: "It is according to the nature
of life that Papageno should be helped on his way by a
hideous old crone on condition that he will marry her. And
it is according to the nature of love that when he agrees she
will turn into a beautiful young girl. But it is according to
the nature of art that both the hideous crone and the beautiful girl are played and sung by the same moderately pretty

38. Nemerov, "Younger Poets: The Lyric Difficulty," in *PF*,
p. 224.

woman of a certain age, who has spent her youth learning music" (11).

Yet, the voice of imagination is not always clearly distinguishable from echo, which is a problem that Nemerov and all true poets have had to contend with since it was first exposed by Plato (*Republic*, X) and Aristotle (*Poetics*, I.2–XVIII) in their widely different theories of mimesis. In another chapter of the *Journal*, Nemerov seeks out his own method of delineating the creative and imitative aspects of imagination. His reflexions turn, dialectially, on the metaphorical notion that "seeing" is the mediator between "the pond" (the mysterious source of imagination) and the art work. This relationship, and the dichotomy it presents, are summarized by the poet:

1. The pond as birthplace and deathplace, the liquid mother and mirror whence beautiful and terrible forms arise, and whereto they return.

2. Artefacts and representations, for example, the portrait of my sister and myself, the Rodin statue and others, the poems I have written about.

3. "Seeing," as mediator between the pond and the art work. Seeing as forbidden and punishable, seeing as protested to be innocent. Photography as the antithesis (guilty) of writing (innocent), and the subsequent revelation that all I said about photography had to be applied word for word to writing as well (*Journal*, 146–47).

Nemerov continues by viewing his basic antithesis (photography/writing) in other terms: science/art ("knowing"/"making"), and imagination/memory—an opposition made also by Stendhal and other writers, as Nemerov acknowledges. He, then, recalls his delight in finding the harmony of science and poetry in the writing of Sir

Charles Sherrington, the eminent neurophysiologist (1857–1952). What particularly attracted Nemerov, because of its brilliance of thought and expression, was a passage from Sherrington's book *Man on His Nature*, which had been reprinted, in essay form, as a memorial in *Scientific American*. In this essay, the making of the eye is described by means of the eye-camera analogy. Aware that Sherrington's metaphors were intrinsic to the imagery of his own poetry, Nemerov records that he copied the following statements from the essay, adding a few thoughts of his own. Taken together, these notations suggest a symbolic equation of mimesis—an equation which brings into focus the poet's basic antithesis and its variants:

"The likeness (of the eye) to an optical camera is plain beyond seeking." If a craftsman making a camera were "told to relinquish wood and metal and glass and to use instead some albumen, salt and water, he certainly would not proceed even to begin." "Water is the great menstruum of 'life.' It makes life possible." "The eye-ball is a little camera." The adjustment of the lens to more or less light in a camera "is made by the observer working the instrument. In the eye this adjustment is automatic, worked by the image itself!"

Particularly striking to me: "all this making of the eye which will see in the light is carried out in the dark. It is a preparing in darkness for use in light."

And: "This living glass-clear sheet is covered with a layer of tear-water constantly renewed. This tear-water has the special chemical power of killing germs which might inflame the eye. This glass-clear bit of skin has only one of the four-fold set of the skin-senses; its touch is always 'pain,' for it should not be touched. . . . And the whole structure, with its pre-science and all its efficiency, is produced by and out of specks of granular slime arranging themselves as of their own accord in sheets and layers, and acting seemingly on an agreed plan" (149–50).

Between these lines, with their juxtaposition of metaphors, the reader can discern a symbolic equation which effects a unity between Nemerov's pairs of opposites: eye/camera = imagination/memory = innocence/guilt = poetry/science ("making"/"knowing") = art/photography. Imagination is analogous to the eye: that which will see in the light is prepared in darkness out of specks of granular slime (out of "the pond," or the unconscious), arranging themselves as if acting on an agreed plan. Imagination is spontaneous. (In the eye, the adjustment of the lens to more or less light is worked by the image itself.) [39] On the other hand, memory is likened to the camera; memory proceeds from the conscious mind. (In the camera, the adjustment of the lens to more or less light is made by the observer working the instrument.) Art, as the creative aspect of vision, is innocent, finding its model (again) in the natural mystery of creation. Photography, as an extension of vision, is imitative and, like memory, records the knowledge of guilt; the camera is "a voyeur," which sees without becoming transformed by the experience.

39. Described here (and indirectly referred to, earlier, by Sherrington) is "accommodation," the eye's ability to focus on objects at varying distances—an ability peculiar to reptiles (except snakes), birds, and mammals. The eye is focused by an adjustment of the shape of the lens, brought about by contraction of the ciliary muscle—an involuntary reflex initiated by the light itself. Changes in the curvature of the lens—and, therefore, the extent to which the lens focuses light—are determined by the degree of contraction of the ciliary muscle. The lens flattens to focus on distant objects and becomes spherical for close objects. The undulating movement of the lens, as accommodation occurs, can rightly be compared to that of the tide—a comparison Nemerov makes in "Runes," XIV. In all respects, the poet's extension of Sherrington's analogy remains a good one.

Although in the light of current scientific research on both the eye and the camera, the eye-camera model is crude, it is still widely used in reputable sources to illustrate the likenesses and differences between the mechanism of the eye and that of the camera. This analogy, as presented by Sherrington and appropriated by Nemerov, remains a valid one, metaphorically speaking, although a scientist, today, might describe the physiology of the eye in more sophisticated terms.

Nemerov concludes his deliberations by stating that "this scientifically accurate and imaginatively convincing story" affected him so powerfully that he "had to relate it at once to the pond, to seeing, to photography, and to art" (*Journal*, 150). He adds that this relation was expressed in the first six lines of "Runes," XIV, which were written before his second reading of Sherrington, "though not certainly before the first." All of "Runes," XIV (which will be analyzed more thoroughly in Chapter 4), is included here as one of Nemerov's most profound poetic illustrations of the creative and imitative aspects of imagination:

> There is a threshold, that meniscus where
> The strider walks on drowning waters, or
> That tensed, curved membrane of the camera's lens
> Which darkness holds against the battering light
> And the distracted drumming of the world's
> Importunate plenty.—Now that threshold,
> The water of the eye where the world walks
> Delicately, is as a needle threaded
> From the reel of a raveling stream, to stitch
> Dissolving figures in a watered cloth,
> A damask either-sided as the shroud
> Of the lord of Ithaca, labored at in light,
> Destroyed in darkness, while the spidery oars
> Carry his keel across deep mysteries
> To harbor in unfathomable mercies.

> (*NSP*, 10)

"Runes," XIV, is also interesting because it is constructed on a type of imagery, used frequently by Nemerov, which, for want of a more precise term, I have called "reflexive." The first six lines above contain two parallel, but antithetical, images—i.e., the two thresholds—which bear an inverse, reflexive relationship to each other. In the last nine lines, the two preceding images have become a single, but paradoxical, image of mind imagining the world. This final image is also an inversion of the first two but succeeds in unifying them. In this poem, as in the entire sequence, a fusion occurs between thought and thing, between figure and meaning, which is accomplished largely through the "reflexive image."

The adjective "reflexive" is used, intentionally, because it has a broader connotative value than its synonym "reflective." Both words convey the "mirror" idea implicit in all imagery. But "reflexive" infers that something not only mirrors an object, or itself, but is also acted upon, or acts upon itself, thereby emitting a response which differs in kind from the stimulus (whether external or internal) and which generates a still different third response but one that retains continuity with all previous responses. The image so conceived is not a duplicate, or negative, or an inversion of an original thing, but is complex, serving connotatively as metaphor and symbol and, equally well, in its own right as the denotation of something. The initial seed and water images in "Runes" have a reflexive continuity through all of their configurations in the poem sequence. Such imagery is powerful because it is organic, multivalent, and capable of reaching human experience on many levels of being.

Reflexive imagery is born from the poet's prismatic lens and is particularly appropriate to the paradoxical complexity of contemporary life. However this type of image is not necessarily new. Certainly John Donne used it often, though it cannot be confined to a metaphysical mode of expression. More modern examples can be found in Yeats' "Among School Children" and "Sailing to Byzantium" and in Wallace Stevens' "Thirteen Ways of Looking at a Blackbird." But reflexive imagery is an intrinsic part of Nemerov's poetry and imaginative process, a means through which the vision and its articulation are one.

Generally, Nemerov's imagery works within a spatial-temporal context which is both circular and linear. As an aspect of vision, this dual dimension of space-time should not be thought of in fixed Euclidian terms but as an artistic extension of Einstein's theory of relativity. More importantly, this double focus on space-time, like the two attitudes voiced in the poems, extends the poet's dual concept of imagination. Human experience is perceived in two ways: ontologically, or substantively, in the circular context, and objectively, or formally, in the linear context. From this duality certain primary paradoxes emerge: darkness/light, eternity/time, the one/the many, substance/form, and actual/ideal, all of which evolve from the poet's fascination with creation and its reverse process, metamorphosis, and the relation, or identity, of the evanescent with the enduring. These basic antitheses are redefined in more immediate paradoxes: mirrors and windows/reality, and statues and effigies/life, both of which paradoxes are contingent upon the divisiveness, fragmentation, complexity, and absurdity of modern existence. Most often the basic antitheses underlie the philosophical, religious poems, whereas the secondary paradoxes find expression in satirical or tragicomic poems which, owing to the poet's sense of dramatic irony, are no less profound.

Paradox is not only the language of poetry but also its province. In his essay "Younger Poets: The Lyric Difficulty" Nemerov writes:

> This difficulty is usually presented to us as a series of pairs of opposites—e.g., form and having something to say, grace and passion, control and urgency, etc. Thus equipped, any man may make his own battlefield, not to mention that h. may also, and probably will, make his own side win. What such warriors of the abstract fail to take into account is that any poet, any at all, is aware that these opposites exist. He is further aware that writing poetry does not mean choosing one side against the other, but achieving the maximum intensity and the greatest harmony of both sides. And

he is painfully aware, from the experience of writing,
that his own temperament (which irremedially belongs
to him, and cannot be subordinated to any ideal however fine) is constantly pushing him toward one side
or the other. But poetry is one of those human activ-
ities in which it is not the object to identify oneself
exclusively with the right or the left, though it is hoped
that the result will look more like tightrope-walking
than fence-sitting (*PF*, 225).

Here again is the problem of the swaying form in its shifting and variable relation to nature and the nature of things
and to the source of great primary human drama, life and
death. That drama begins in the garden where relations
grow; outside the garden is the vast abyss—the eternal
mystery beyond the reach of prophecy or parable. In contemplating this situation in the mirror of language, Nemerov proceeds from the hypothesis that God exists, however
doubtful man's relationship and communication with Him
has become. The problem of relating and communicating is
that of imagination itself—imagination which becomes central to the universe and the most important thing to understand about the universe precisely because it has become
problematic and doubtful. In this respect, poetry is for
Nemerov not only a way of being but an act of faith, a leap
into the unknown.

The complexity of Nemerov's position, as a man and
as a poet, is best articulated in an off-the-cuff statement he made in a letter to Robert D. Harvey, a statement
which provides also a fitting summary of the poet's concept
of poetry and its purpose. "Poetry is a kind of spiritual
exercise, a (generally doomed but stoical) attempt to pray
one's humanity back into the universe; and conversely an
attempt to read, to derive anew, one's humanity from nature, nature considered as a book, a dictionary and bible
at once. Poetry is a doctrine of signatures, or presupposes
that the universe is such a doctrine whether well written

or ill. . . . Poetry is an art of combination, or discovering the secret valencies which the most widely differing things have for one another. In the darkness of this search, patience and good humour are useful qualities. Also: the serious and funny are one. The purpose of poetry is to persuade, fool or compel God into speaking."[40]

Reading Nemerov, one is reminded that the sublime and terrible treasure that was lost may yet exist in unfathomed seas where a poet of another time and place will find it transformed "into something rich and strange." If Nemerov has not claimed it, he has at least sounded in those waters.

40. Robert D. Harvey, "A Prophet Armed," pp. 125–26.

2

THE RUNNING WATER
AND THE STANDING STONE

For NEMEROV, the initiatory ascent from earth
through water and air to fire is precariously balanced between what is temporal and spatial (form) and what is enduring (substance). This ascent, though it can be traced
throughout the poet's work, should be regarded primarily
as part of a metaphorical, rather than a developmental
or biographical, pattern. All of his elemental images are
so integrated that separation is impossible, but, from their
consistent use, a poetic vocabulary can be discerned with
its unique idioms and natural symbols. The early poems are
more earthbound in subject matter, which facilitates the
natural grouping of earth and water images with the antithesis of statues and effigies/life and creation. Similarly,
air (space) and fire (light), which are most apparent in the
later poems, can be appropriately grouped with the antithesis of mirrors and windows/reality and will be studied in
Chapter 3. Nevertheless, such divisions are arbitrary, since
all images are correlated throughout the poet's work and
the ascent is not a historical process: it repeats itself, in
different contexts, and follows a circular pattern, finding
its natural parallel in the rhythm of the seasons and the
ebb and flow of the tides.

The most astute observation of Nemerov's use of earth and water imagery is made by the poet himself in "Attentiveness and Obedience": "In . . . 'A Spell before Winter,' I spoke of 'the running water and the standing stone.' This distinction of imagery goes far and deep in my poetry and has assumed, over the past seven years, the nature of an antithesis. Long before writing that poem, I had observed in my work a growing preoccupation with statues, with heroic monuments, as representing the rigid domination of the past over present and future: stillness, death, power, compacted into giant forms; the standing stone that looks over the landscape assumes early in history a human face, a frown, even a smile; becomes a God" (246–47).

In Nemerov's poetry, statues and monuments symbolize the weight of man's bondage to earth and his swift return to dust. These artifacts of earth and stone also represent "a false, historical immorality" which the poet associates with the second commandment of the Mosaic Law, the prohibition against making graven images. From statues and monuments Nemerov derives a broader category of earth-centered imagery which he refers to as "effigies." This category includes photographs, heirlooms, souvenirs, mythological types (such as Santa Claus), cartoon characters, mannequins in shop windows, and all things which impose on the mind a habit of viewing the world in a sterile, idolatrous way. Even newspapers and television are effigies of a kind, in the sense that they imprint verbal and visual images on people's minds day after day and, in so doing, confirm human beings in the habit of regarding these representations as the only reality.[1] In many of his poems, Nemerov contends that the world, with increasing acceleration, is becoming impounded in its own idolatry through a proliferation of graven images, the model for which is the statue, or the standing stone.

The opposite attitude is "attentiveness and obedience."

1. Nemerov, "Attentiveness and Obedience," p. 248.

Antithetical to the image of stone is that of "running water—so dialectical, so subtle, so strange, and yet so evidently an emblem of human life and the life of the imagination—of a stream, a river, a waterfall, a fountain, or else of a still and deep-reflecting pool. This image of the form continuing in the changing material belongs to cloud and fire, and I once gave it a somewhat political shape in a despairing epigram: God loves (I said) the liberal thrice better than the conservative, for at the beginning he gave to the liberal the three realms of water, air, and fire, while to the conservative he gave only the earth."[2]

However, as the poet acknowledges, the solids and the liquids of this world are both essential and define each other. The stream is known by its rocky bed; the rocks direct the water's flow just as the water, slowly and secretly, shapes the rocks according to its flow. Yet the poet admits to accentuating the liquids, probably because the world "continues to worship the rocky monument achieved and scorns the spring, the rain cloud and the spark fallen among leaves."[3]

The rejection of the solids of the world seems credible in a poet whose interest in nature is not a practical one and who has known the fresh, various beauty of New England's seacoast, hills, woods, and springs. A prairie poet, like Carl Sandburg, or a poet of the Pacific Coast, like Robinson Jeffers, finds majesty in rock, canyon, and earth. But for Nemerov, earth and stone are synonymous with man's ancient burden—his frustration and struggle against time. In "The Quarry,"[4] man, who is so often portrayed as plunderer of the land, is seen as its victim. The futility of man's painstaking efforts, as a civilized creature, to halt or repair the ravages of time turns inward to become the dry wound of despair and emptiness:

2. Ibid., p. 250.
3. Ibid.
4. In *SG*, p. 74; and *NSP*, p. 40. A similar attitude is expressed

> . . . Long silent years
> Have split the walls that men with crowbars
> And blast had split before; and all repairs
> —I know it now—but ravage and ruin again
> For the life's sake. The stone and vine-grown crater
> I stare on, my dry wound in nature,
> Is absence everywhere.

The "stone" is an inversion of the biblical meaning, for it signifies the impossibility of faith in a meaningless world. The "vine-grown crater" has biblical echoes; God's people (the vine) planted, in this instance, on bad soil, struggle to survive but are choking themselves out of existence for want of water, the source of life. This image is reinforced by the juxtaposition of stone (compact, brute male force) and its supplemental feminine image, the dry crater, or womb, from which the struggling vines proliferate, only to decompose in a short time, for, as the poet says:

> what curbs or schools
> Or monuments were squared by such rude rules,
> Quarried and carried away and dressed in line,
> Before the stone could be split by the tree,
> And the tree brought down by the vine.

Whereas "The Quarry" represents the natural process as one of deterioration and the loss of identity, "The Town Dump"[5] shows death and decay as a necessary part of the regenerative process against which man's pitiable attempts to conserve his dead past, or preserve his identity, appear ludicrous and strange. As the subtitle (taken from Shakespeare) indicates, "The art of our necessities is strange / That can make vile things precious" (*King Lear*, 3.2.70–

---

in "A Day on the Big Branch," in *MW*, pp. 13–16; and *NSP*, pp. 93–96.

5. In *MW*, pp. 5–6; and *NSP*, pp. 89–90.

71). While the external situation is internalized in "The Quarry," the reverse happens here. The town dump is "the garbage dump of the self," as the poet tells us in the *Journal* (181–82) in a passage which infers that the "objects of value or virtue" in the poem are the deadwood of man's past thoughts and actions—the so-called "visible" results of a life—which he would redeem in the form of mottoes, slogans, and instructions to the future.

In the figure of the poem, the dump is the city returning to nature (decay), in apposition to the cemetery on the hillside where the inhabitants are likewise returning to dust. In the town dump, man scavenges to find "objects of value or virtue"—"family pearls" thrown out by accident, "Derelict chairs which will turn out to be / By Hepplewhite," lacquered cups, and other refuse of the past, which man has made, revered, and tries to redeem. But the flies are there, too, as the destructive energy which preserves the ecological balance. Nemerov pictures them as "A dynamo / Composed, by thousands, of our ancient black Retainers," who have served the world by restoring man's debris to its elemental state so that nature is constantly renewed. The flies are the most vivid and vital image in the poem. One hears their hum, "steady / As someone telling beads, the hum becoming / A high whine at any disturbance"; and "they shine under the sun / Like oil-drops, or are invisible as night, / By night." They are dark manifestations of the solar energy which continuously moves, mostly invisibly, throughout a world in which nothing finishes. They signify, too, the energetic principle by which the self exists each day until its form is spent.

Yet civilized man, alienated from his natural source, cannot relate to or identify with the dynamic process in himself and in nature, as the end of the poem implies. Always man must justify energy in terms of finished results or explain it according to ratios. "You may sum up / The results, if you want results," the poet tells us, with the in-

ference that ratios and results have little connection with
the nature of things in an unfinished world:

> . . . But I will add
> That wild birds, drawn to the carrion and flies,
> Assemble in some numbers here, their wings
> Shining with light, their flight enviably free,
> Their music marvelous, though sad, and strange.

While the human predicament in the poem can be (and
has been) viewed in various ways, interpretation involves
the problem of freedom and necessity as it interrelates with
the problem of identity. Though less dramatic, the predicament of "The Town Dump" is that of Lear on the heath,
as the subtitle suggests, and is also played out in a chaotic,
elemental setting. Lear, as we see him in act 3, is exiled
from his past and stripped of his royal trappings (the su-
perficial emblems which identify him). Exposed to the war-
ring elements without and within, his struggle revolves
on the loss of identity as it relates to the problem of freedom
and necessity.

But, whereas Lear's predicament is resolved, there is
no resolution in "The Town Dump." In his struggle between
freedom and necessity man has emerged his own prisoner,
bound by the small necessities he has artifacted—the material objects, mottoes, and emblems through which he
would preserve himself and which he uses and discards at
will. Divided within, he has lost his identity, which, ironi-
cally, he tries to redeem among the flies and the smoldering
refuse of the human junkyard. Though fascinated by the
invisible relationship between "the flies," "the purifying
fires" (smoldering garbage), and "the hunters by night,"
the poet nevertheless refuses to reduce reality—being and
becoming—to ratios and results. A sense of wonder remains
as his imagination moves on to the flocks of wild birds,
"drawn to the carrion and flies." Like the dynamo of flies

(which, "feeling the heat, keep on the move"), the birds
are creatures of necessity—spontaneous expressions of a
universal energy and rhythm unknown to man. Their wings
shine with light and their flight is "enviably free," so that,
for the briefest instant, the poet seems to escape human
bondage and be caught up with them as part of the dynamic
process. Yet, even here, nothing is resolved, for identification is incomplete; the music of the birds, however marvelous, "is sad, and strange."

The pathos of the human situation is heard in the
poet's voice as it shifts casually in the last five lines from
that of the detached witty commentator to a more serious
tone. These lines rise and fall musically with the flight of
the birds and with the poet's mood as it lifts for a magical
moment, then drops suddenly, leaving us with an inexplicable sense of loss and estrangement. This mood is characteristic of Nemerov's early poems and can be associated
with his desire to find again the lost vision that was Shakespeare's. In the paragraph that follows "The Town Dump"
passage in the *Journal* Nemerov reveals this desire in words
which further illuminate what has been said about the
poem: "Only now, for instance, when I have resolved to
put away this work [the *Journal*] for an indefinite time,
the thought comes to me that the predicaments of my most
characteristic and intimate imagery strangely belong to
Shakespeare too, who resolved them by magical poetry in
his Last Plays. May it happen to me also one day that the
statue shall move and speak, and the drowned child be
found, and the unearthly music sing to me" (182).

Perhaps what Nemerov is contesting, in his search for a
unitive vision, is man's mirror of nature. The standing stone
looking over the landscape may symbolize death, power, and
stillness because it has assumed, throughout history, human
features which man has deified in his faith and art. Nemerov's response to rock and barren earth extends even more
negatively to the artifacts of civilization and history, which

continue to hold a rigid and fatal domination over us. Our idolatry toward material objects is enforced through history, which inscribes death in books, on monuments, and on our consciences. History, in fact, is a forgery of life, as "To Clio, Muse of History" (*NRD*, 3–4) tells us:

> One more casualty
> One more screen memory penetrated at last
> To be destroyed in the endless anamnesis
> Always progressing, never arriving at a cure.
> My childhood in the glare of that giant form
> Corrupts with history, for I too fought in the war.

The poem depicts the Etruscan Warrior (having been proved a forgery), who represents the thrust of male power which continues to seduce us with its lie about life, making itself a god. Note the sardonic twist given the biblical phrase (used in the burial rite), "The Lord hath given, and the Lord hath taken away":

> . . . History has given
> And taken away; murders become memories,
> And memories become the beautiful obligations:
> As with a dream interpreted by one still sleeping,
> The interpretation is only the next room of the dream.

The perverse effect of history on man's attitudes is underscored in the final verse when the poet recalls how "we children" used to stare at the statue, learning "unspeakable things about war" (which aren't in books), and that his photographs, sold in the Metropolitan Museum, were in full color, "With the ancient genitals blacked out."

Statues, effigies, and mythological heroes are hollow forms, or abstractions, of what once was; they say nothing of the truth of existence. The disparity between what is actual and the ideals we cherish is the theme of "The Statues in the Public Gardens" (*MW*, 11–12; *NSP*, 53–54) :

> In darker glades, the nearly naked stone
> Of athlete, goddess chaste as any snows
> That stain them winters, tempts maiden and man
> From their prosthetic immortality:
> Pythagoras' thigh, or Tycho's golden nose,
> For a figleaf fallen from the withered tree.

The statue, a cold fragment of a former life, or of an imagined life, is history's lie about the pitiable human condition. In the *Journal* (170) Nemerov writes: "The idea of statues, connected with the biblical prohibition of graven images, entered my poetry slowly at first, perhaps seven years ago ('The Statues in the Public Gardens'), but recently with more frequency and force, so that a third of the poems in my latest book could be grouped together under the general name of *Effigies*, including by analogy with the form and function of statues such metaphorical extensions as photographs, Santa Claus, mannequins in shop windows, snowmen, famous and influential people, and even the unsuccessful heroes turned to stone by the Gorgon's head. . . ."

In the subsequent paragraph of the *Journal*, Nemerov relates "rigidity, death, erection, in the 'statuesque' thought of paralysis and helplessness." He adds that "statues cannot move, yet they move us by example; they represent impotence and omnipotence simultaneously." The poet's irreverent attitude toward the traditionally respected work of art is humorously thrust into an epigram, "Don Juan to the Statue" (*NRD*, 10) :

> Dominant marble, neither will I yield!
> The soul endures at one with its election,
> Lover to bed or soldier to the field,
> Your daughter's the cause of this & that erection.

In rejecting the statuesque and the historical, Neme-

rov is repudiating not only the rigid domination of the past
but also a mirror of nature that is purely visual, recording
only the surfaces of things and the erosive effects of time.
Beyond art, myth, legend, and all that is bracketed in time,
is the other side of history, the dark impenetrable silence
which, when lit by language, casts a shadow of truth—a
shadow perceptible only as it is actual in the here and now.
"Deep Woods" is a journey to the edge of this deeper reality, a retreat experienced by the inner self in nature's interior. Like many of Nemerov's poems which explore the
problem of mimesis, "Deep Woods"[6] begins soberly and
turns out to be a *reductio ad absurdum*, though one which
is accomplished with such wit, balance, and timing that the
effect is profoundly serious as well as hilariously funny.
The experience begins as both an escape and a venture—a
frenzied but essential move from the beaten track of time
into the unknown:

> Such places are too still for history,
> Which slows, shudders, and shifts as the trucks do,
> In hearing-distance, on the highway hill,
> And staggers onward elsewhere with its load
> Of statues, candelabra, buttons, gold;
> But here the heart, racing strangely as though
> Ready to stop, reaches a kind of rest. . . .

Yet, in the primeval, uncharted forest, the mind rests un-
easily and, like a hunted beast, makes "tiredness and ter-
ror / Its camouflage," then falls asleep and dreams. The
dream is of being lost, covered with leaves, and "hidden
in a death like any sleep / So deep the bitter world must
let it be / And go bay elsewhere after better game."
     This feeling of being hunted down, followed by a vol-
untary, or desired, "fall" and "going under," appears frequently, though with variation, in Nemerov's poems. Usu-

6. In *SG,* pp. 81–83; and *NSP,* pp. 97–99.

ally the fall results in a loss of self-awareness (reflexivity) through which regeneration, identity, or insight occurs. But, here, the mind remains always one step removed from the external and internal reality with which it would merge. The experience is "a dream of being lost" and "hidden in a death like any sleep," and it is a wakeful sleep at that. Though subject and object, time, space, and motion are distorted as in a dream (lines 8–11), the restless eye continues to reflect, turning upon itself, as elemental nature is revealed in endless profusion without logic, continuity, or relationship (lines 16–20).

In the deep woods the restless eye meets only indifference. All that ever was and ever will be is here now; "Line, leaf, and light; darkness invades our day. . . ." Paradox, meaning, pattern, and drama—all that man abstracts out of time—are nonexistent here. Even death is delayed, having no name:

> . . . Even the giant oak,
> Stricken a hundred years or yesterday,
> Has not found room to fall as heroes should
> But crookedly leans on an awkward-squad of birch,
> The tragic image and the mighty crash
> Indefinitely delayed in favor of
> Fresh-weaving of vines, rooting of outer branches,
> Beginning again, in spaces still more cramped,
> A wandering calligraphy which seems
> Enthralled to a magic constantly misspelled.

These woods, though timeless, are also once in time, bearing nature's inscriptions, here and now, in a language no man can decipher:

> . . . These here are the deep woods
> Of now, New England, this October, when

Dry gold has little left to change, and half
The leaves are gone to ground, and half of those
Rained in the leaf-mold which tenses in
The fastenings of frost; where the white branches
Of birch are dry bones airborne in assaults
Which haven't worked yet.

Here, the natural process follows no rule except its own,
nor can it be rendered in any iconic form by imagination.
This is an unlegended land—"no Black Forest where the
wizard lived," nor "the hot swamp theatrical with snakes /
And tigers; nor the Chinese forest on / The mountainside,
with bridge, pagoda, fog, / Three poets in the foreground
drinking tea. . . ." Nemerov adds, parenthetically, that
"there is no tea and not so many as three." Man's attempts
to spell himself into and out of these woods appear ridicu-
lous. "What is" defines itself; this is a land,

                                    unmitigated by myth
And whose common splendors are comparable only to
Themselves; this leaf, line, light, are scrawled alone
In solar definitions on a lump
Of hill like nothing known since Nature was
Invented by Watteau or Fragonard
In the Old Kingdom or the time of Set
Or before the Flood of Yao (or someone else
Of the same name) in the Fourth, or Disney, Dimension.

The concluding stanza paints a satiric portrait of
human history, filled with wit and irony, although the humor
is not acerbic since the poet has emerged from the experience in the deep woods as one of us. In his attempt to frame
that experience in the mirror of language, he has come
face to face with his own image and can only laugh. The
opening lines of this stanza are a parody on human vanity.

Having shown us the raw material of creation, the world before the Fall, the poet speaks, with a biblical echo:

> And this is yours to work; plant it to salt
> Or men in armor who destroy each other,
> Sprinkle with dragon's blood early in spring
> And see what happens, epic or pastoral. . . .

And he goes on to say that, probably, nothing will happen: "This / Place is too old for history to know / Beans about." Through a succession of clever allusions to myth, legend, and recorded literature, he traces man's efforts to inscribe the darkness back to the beginning of time. All such efforts are as nothing against the slow intransigence of these silent woods which shadow the deeper reality:

> The other Ahasuerus has not spat
> Nor walked nor cobbled any shoe, nor Joseph
> So much as dreamed that he will found the Corn
> Exchange Bank in the baked country of Egypt.
> Not even those burnt beauties are hawked out,
> By the angry Beginner, on Chaos floor
> Where they build Pandemonium the Palace
> Back in the high old times. Most probably
> Nothing will happen. Even the Fall of Man
> Is waiting, here, for someone to grow apples;
> And the snake, speckled as sunlight on the rock
> In the deep woods, still sleeps with a whole head
> And has not begun to grow a manly smile.

In "Deep Woods," as in most of Nemerov's earthbound poems, no resolution occurs if, by "resolution," we mean a merging of the mind with the deeper reality. Nature remains indifferent and unresponsive to language; never does the mind, even fleetingly, submerge. Yet the experience is too real to leave us unchanged; some insight is gained and our perception is sharpened. Perhaps we see, as D. H. Lawrence did, how a snake actually looks, "speckled as sunlight on the rock / In the deep woods. . . ." We may also recognize that the predicaments of the poet's imagery belong, not so strangely, to Shakespeare too, rather than to Thoreau, who might have given them a more unitive, if not a happier, ending. The problem confronted in the poem is that of "Single Nature's double name," intensified here to become "single nature's triple name." The magical number "three" riddles the poem, although nature defines itself always in singular terms. In the deep woods, "this leaf, line, light, are scrawled alone / In solar definitions on a lump / Of hill. . . ." While we can never decipher the "wandering calligraphy which seems / Enthralled to a magic constantly misspelled," we are able to see with greater clarity and to view these woods as they really are—"the deep woods / Of now, New England, this October. . . ."

The poet reminds us again that his task, unlike that of the historian, is to name a situation that he himself is in. He must name what is actual, immediate, and particular in order to illuminate the interval between past and future. If history formalizes experience and commemorates the past, nature does not; and it is in nature that Nemerov seeks his model of the creative process and its reverse, metamorphosis, or the relation of the evanescent (form) with the enduring (substance). However Nemerov regards the solids of this world, he still recognizes the essential relation between form and substance and the way in which each is defined by the other. This invisible relation, for which the natural paradigm is the seashell and the sea, is spun out in the poem "Shells." Skillfully integrated aurally and visually, the poem winds like a shell from beginning to end, a circular study of form itself.

Initially, the shell is presented as a hollow form— empty, light, and dry—which can be picked up on the shore and leaves a powdery chalk on the hands. "The life

that made it is gone out." It is the shell of a former self, as
people say,

> Failing to take into account
> The vital waste in composition
> With the beauty of the ruined remainder. . . .
>
> (*MW*, 9–11; *NSP*, 91–92)

Such an empty form is useless, of course, except as a decora-
tion, "A Souvenir of Sunset Beach, etc." As an abstraction,
the shell is "only cryptically / Instructive, if at all: it
winds / Like generality, from nothing to nothing / By means
of nothing but itself." Emblematic of "the steep ascent,"
of all abstract, logical, and historical concepts, it "is a stair-
way going nowhere. . . ."

Pure form, as a hollow shell, mocks us with its echo—
"the obedient sounds of waters / Beat by your Mediterranean, classic heart, / In bloody tides as long as breath," or
the pulsing of our own blood in the shell of the ear. Yet
form defines and is defined by what it is not: the echo of
Mediterranean waters (the bloodstream), of tides which
have ebbed and flooded "Upon the ruining house of histories,"

> Whose whitening stones, in Africa,
> Bake dry and blow away, in Athens,
> In Rome, abstract and instructive as chalk
> When children scrawl the blackboard full
> Of wild spirals every which way,
> To be erased with chalk dust, then with water.

The shell, which has had symbolic significance since
antiquity among many different cultures, provides the classical example of pure form and works well as a reflexive
image within the poem. The shell, defined by Mediterranean waters, is reflected in the form of the ear where,

through the pulsing of the blood, images come into being from forms of the classical world. The auricle of the ear is, in turn, reflected in the spirals scrawled on the blackboard in chalk, "To be erased with chalk dust, then with water." Though nothing is lost in nature, the poet makes it clear that the liquids of the world are what, ultimately, endure.

The relation of earth and water becomes a central theme in the poems of *The Salt Garden*, which mark a crossing point in Nemerov's development as a man and a poet. The poems, many of which share a similar imagery pattern, take the shape of a philosophical inquiry, as the poet seeks his identity, trying to discover where he has been and where he is going.

Robert D. Harvey observes, with some insight, that three important experiences come through Nemerov's early poems: "the city childhood, the wartime violence, and the impact after these of nature—the sea and the Vermont hills. . . ."[7] Harvey cites such poems as "Redeployment," "The Soldier Who Lived through the War," and "Life Cycle of the Common Man" as indicating that, even after the experience of war, life is seen "as either dangerous and contingent and vital, or a vacant drift to nothingness." As Harvey puts it, the "dangers of commitment to the chaos of 'reality' are the same every way, but facing these dangers, accepting the commitment, is what constitutes life." Nemerov's imagination draws on war, city, and nature and, in his later verse, conflict is expressed in the "endless struggle between city and nature, between mind and world."[8]

Certainly, conflict appears in Nemerov's work but, mainly, as an extension of the total vision that paradox exists in all phenomena. In *The Salt Garden*, the city-nature complex goes deep, as Harvey notes. But, this complex, conveyed chiefly through related earth and sea images, is only one manifestation of the poet's broader

7. "A Prophet Armed," p. 117.
8. Ibid., p. 120.

concern for the relation between the evanescent and enduring. The view in *The Salt Garden* (41–43) is of man
working, "with an amateur's toil," "much patience," and
"some sweat," to create a pleasant greenery

> From a difficult, shallow soil
> That, now inland, was once the shore
> And once, maybe, the ocean floor.

Man watches his accomplishments bend in the salt wind so
that he becomes aware of the mighty though distant ocean.

The salt garden is the garden of the world, or of civilization—paradoxical, mutable, a simultaneous process of
life and death. Indefinite as to exact location and point in
time, the garden is somewhere between the city and the sea,
partaking of both. Thus, the garden may be viewed from
three perspectives, all of which are interrelated. On one
level, the garden circumscribes some evolutionary point in
time when man exists in limbo between his sea origins and
his political civilization. The implications of this setting
are reinforced by the lack of what is commonly called
"progress" in the garden. The inland place, which was
"once the shore / And once, maybe the ocean floor," produces nothing that does not bend with the salt wind. In
another way, the garden is extremely concrete—a particular place and time in the poet's life in which the younger
urban man is becoming an older lover of nature, or moving
back to his origins. The produce of the garden is comparable to the poet's work, his creativity and his productivity.
The active gardener stands back to survey the fruits of his
labor. From a third point of view, the garden is internal, a
state of mind or being in which the poet seeks to formulate
what he is and what life ultimately means to a "tenant
gardener." All of the parables point to Adam after the
Fall.

The related earth and water images bear out the meaning on all three levels. Earth signifies mutability, even though, for a while, it has replaced the ocean. But it is the salt sea—generative, destructive, and regenerative—that will endure. Thus, "Turnip and bean and violet / In a decent order set, / Grow, flourish and are gone. . . ." Even a civilized pride exists in the "ruins of stalk and shell, / The vine when it goes brown," and these things "die well." Yet the salt wind is always there and "The ocean's wrinkled green / Maneuvers in its sleep. . . ."

In the gull image, of the second half of the poem, Harvey finds a suggestion of Yeats' wild swan (and rightly so) but with Nemerov's stamp upon it: "What emerges for the city man's awareness from his encounter with the great gull is an inexplicable sense of identity with the bird. Men build cities and so become human. But in becoming human they enter upon the hazards of moral life. In emerging from and building ramparts against 'nature,' whatever that is, they lose their innocence—in a word, they 'fall.' "[9] This separation is the fall of man; the contact with the bird, man's salvation. Harvey states that the feeling of helplessness and nonentity, while seeming to be an invalid response to this encounter, is not completely denied in the poem's resolution. Man's garden is sown with salt; therefore his only hope (and a limited one) is that, through his own efforts, he can make the garden somewhat green. But beyond the moral and philosophical meanings that Harvey draws, there is the humanness of that response to the encounter, so fleeting and elusive. Man sorrows because he cannot transcend himself, because he *is* a "tenant gardener," with feet of clay, and cannot find the freedom he has lost except in the moment of identity, which is, paradoxically, the moment of self-submission—the moment of revelation. In the great gull Nemerov sees "fierce austerity," a savage freedom and

9. Ibid., p. 121. Nemerov's description of the encounter with the gull is also reminiscent of Hart Crane's encounter with the same wild bird in the proem "To Brooklyn Bridge."

pride, but it is pride before the Fall, before civilization began. The gull is "that image of the wild / Wave where it beats the air" which has come "To teach the tenant gardener, / Green Fellow of this paradise, / Where his salt dreams lie."

Man's separation from himself and from nature must inevitably bring him back to his sea origins, or water, as the source of life and symbol of purification, or regeneration. Water and light are Nemerov's strongest elemental images and, though their meanings are frequently similar, they generally signify the life of the body and the mind, respectively. Both water and light are used separately and together as metaphors for the imagination.

The analogy between salt sea—salt vine and the blood-stream and veins is frequent in Nemerov's poems and provides a good example of the reflexive image with its multivalent meanings. Nemerov, as Kenneth Burke notes,[10] is quick to grasp the visual, audial, and connotative similarities between words like "vine" and "vein." Such words are always used in contexts where their plurisignitive meanings come into play, sometimes paradoxically. Thus, the salt sea, which is the source of life, is also destructive; besides erosion and decomposition, the sea brings tidal waves and floods upon "the ruining house of histories." Consequently, man views the ocean in many ways, often attributing to it the moral qualities of good and evil. But, for Nemerov, the sea is infinite substance, beyond good and evil. His perspective is biblical, for he regards water as a creative and purifying force, a means of regeneration and renewal. "Water is the menstruum of life" (*Journal*, 149). Through water life is born, through the tear-glass of the eye imagination springs, and through the flood is purgation. Such a force sanctifies that which it permeates and recreates, for all objects are but fleeting forms on the changing surface of eternity.

10. "Comments on Eighteen Poems by Howard Nemerov," p. 121.

Science, with faith, substantiates the salt sea–salt vine and bloodstream-vein analogy. Rachel Carson tells us that each land animal is linked to its origin in the sea: "Fish, amphibian, and reptile, warm-blooded bird and mammal— each of us carries in our veins a salty stream in which the elements sodium, potassium, and calcium are combined in almost the same proportions as in sea water. This is our inheritance from the day . . . when a remote ancestor, having progressed from the one-celled to the many-celled stage, first developed a circulatory system in which the fluid was merely the water of the sea."[11] Man, composed largely of water (roughly 80%), is indeed a microcosm. The salt in his system, besides preserving the water balance, modulates body temperature, preserves the flesh, and purifies the blood. The connection between salt sea and bloodstream is a valid one.

Likewise, the analogy between "vine" and "vein" can be established on both a metaphorical and scientific basis. God compared his people to a vine (when he brought them out of Egypt), which he planted in Palestine, as being good soil. But His people turned to the golden calf, and the vines produced bitter grapes.[12] Vine, as a synonym for the living flesh, is used often in both the Old and New Testaments. Apart from their obvious visible similarities, veins, like vines, require air, water, and light.

While "The Scales of the Eyes"[13] will be discussed in greater detail in the next chapter, certain passages can be cited, out of context, in which this basic water-blood analogy is used. This particular poem, which is an argosy of the poet, synthesizes many of his dominant images, some of which have already been discussed. The following lines are a parable of the city, the earthbound world, where man,

11. *The Sea around Us*, pp. 13–14.
12. Psalms 80:8; and Isaiah 5:1.
13. In *SG*, pp. 21–38; and *NSP*, pp. 61–71.

removed from his source, no longer commits himself to
life:

> Dead men in their stone towns
> Wait out the weather lying down,
> And spread widely underground
> The salt vines of blood.

In contrast to the city is the sea:

> Out there beyond the island
> The sea pounds a free way through,
> Her wide tides spread on the sand
> Stick and brine and rolling stone
> The long weather long.

In addition to salt and the vine (which cannot grow underground), there are further echoes of the doomed cities of
the Bible which support the meaning of these symbols. The
city beneath his foot, "the secret beast," is a "white lion
among waters, / Who settest thy claw upon the time." The
city is a place where "The bees hum / The honeyed doom
of time and time / Again, and riddle this underground /
How sweetness comes from the great strength."

The source of this figure is Samson's Riddle (Judges
14:8–14). In explicating this passage, Kenneth Burke says
that the city "is perhaps condemned for its dark strivings,
but its time-mindedness seems almost like an accent of
eternity (and above all, we insist, it figures moods not alien
but integral to the poet)." On the basis of Nemerov's constant time/eternity antithesis, this passage does not appear
to accent eternity in any way. However, the moods figured
are certainly integral to the poet in the context of the early
sections of the poem. As Burke says, there is a pattern of
inversion throughout the poem, and, "if the moods of the

Self are translated into corresponding imagery of sensation, then the duplication without can be experienced as imposing itself upon the sensibilities of the experiencer." This appears to be true, and the image of the lion, above, finds its corresponding but converse image later on in the sequence (in IX) where the poet's mood is more accurately identified with the sea:

> Striding and turning, the caged sea
> Knocks at the stone and falls away,
> Will not rest night or day
> Pacing to be free.
>
> The spiral shell, held at the ear,
> Hums the ocean or the blood
> A distant cry, misunderstood
> Of the mind in the coiled air.

The duality in these images corresponds to the poet's mood—the dark throes of the dilemma. The following first verse of "The Scales of the Eyes," X, bears this out. Again, the consistency of the poet's unique natural symbols is evident:

> Roads lead to the sea, and then?
> The signs drown in the blowing sand,
> The breathing and smoothing tide.
> It has been a long journey so far.
> Gull, where do I go now?

Another water image, which appears in *The Salt Garden* and in subsequent poems, is the pond. Nemerov is fascinated by this "miniature world . . . small enough to be observed and reported by a single intelligence, a kind of natural art work. But also a teeming full creation, growing every year more wild, more fierce with life, more manifold in species, exfoliating a domestic jungle not without its sinister aspect, connected with the amount of killing that goes on there through the summer days."[14]

The pond symbolizes to the poet the childhood or source of his art. He sees the pond "as birthplace and death place, the liquid mother and mirror whence beautiful and terrible forms arise and whereto they return."[15] The pond is analogous to the unconscious, to the secret beginnings of art, and again, to the dark, slimy granules out of which the eye is constructed. The pond is literally and figuratively the source of imagination.

The poet declares that he, himself, has also killed in the pond when he "drowned a child named the Christ Bearer,[16] whose name was given the pond, and whose death is thus heroic . . . so that he became the eponymous ancestor of all that multitudinous life and death." The poem is about naming, the poet explains, and "connects the art of poetry itself with naming, naming with sacrifice. In identifying the art of poetry with naming I say my own name (the poet is the namer of the world)."[17]

The imagery associated with "The Pond" is reflexive in the passive and active sense. The poet's own words serve best to describe these associations. "Seeking a metaphoric expression of it, rejecting 'machine,' I said it was a fire. Later on, an oil fire (on account of the oily blackness of its surface). Allusions to fire: the children with matches, the sun (son) drowned in the pond and burning there, burning gold. The fire of life 'turning its inward heat upon itself.' Also as a city (Skoplje?) : The creatures 'peopled thick the city of themselves.' I remember, too, a theory that life began, not in the sea as often supposed, but in fresh-water

14. *Journal*, pp. 107–8.
15. Ibid., p. 146.
16. "The Pond," in *SG*, pp. 14–18; *NSP*, pp. 42–46; and *Journal*, pp. 185–89.
17. *Journal*, p. 108.

ponds. Taking these references together with what has
already been said on this subject, it begins to appear that the
pond is the Mother . . ." (*Journal* 109–10).

The poet adds that another association is that of a
fable that he had once made up, in which the drowned
Narcissus "speaks about poetry as the contemplation of, the
dying into, the imagery of the pond."[18]

Conversely, the poet also sees the pond as the source
of "variously malformed lives," which relates it to "The
Mud Turtle," who "takes a secret wound out of the world"
(*BS*, 98). In this poem, the turtle comes from the very
depths of the pond, from the mud, and makes his pilgrimage
to sunlight—a dark lord who comes from hell and climbs
out of the darkness to the height and then goes down like
the sun. The secret wound is our guilt for the turtle's ampu-
tated foot, "as though he momentarily revealed to us something horrifyingly bitten and lost beneath the foundation
of the world. . . ." The turtle shows us a view of "a natural
thing" and is emblematic of "the kingdom of darkness with
its implacable hurt," which leaves us fascinated but bewil-
dered.[19] The poet sees something chivalrous in the turtle's
armor (his shell) and some majestic quality and pride in
his natural filth. Like the gull, the turtle signifies what we
have lost in the civilizing process. But, whereas the gull
suggests soul or mind transcending the body, the turtle is
identified directly with the body and the pond, the primitive
unconscious, and the fantastic world of childhood, of fairy
tales and imagining. The poet's explication of "The Pond"
and "The Mud Turtle" is all-inclusive, replete with Freu-
dian symbols, which serve only to bridge some gap in time.
What came first and what remains is the mystery of the
pond, whence emerges the turtle, lord of darkness, and the
dragonfly, "a winged animal of light," who, "before it could
delight the eye, had been / In a small way a dragon of the

18. Ibid., p. 116.
19. Ibid., pp. 131–32.

deep, / A killer and meat-eater on the floor / Beneath the
April surface of the pond";

> it rose and cast its kind in May
> As though putting away costume and mask
> In the bitter play, and taking a lighter part.

Somewhere between the ocean, which reflects eternity,
and the still pond, which reflects self, are the raindrops and
the snowfall. Rain, when configured with spring, light, and
regeneration, is beautiful, as in the last poem of "The
Scales of the Eyes." The first and third of three verses are
included here:

> Of leaf and branch and rain and light,
> The spider's web glistened with wet,
> The robin's breast washed red in sun
> After the rapid storm goes on;
>
> *   *   *   *   *   *   *   *   *
>
> New happiness of everything!
> The blind worm lifts up his head
> And the sparrow shakes a wet wing
> In the home of little while.

In these lines it is almost impossible to separate water and
sun. If any poet has ever caught the fresh, wet loveliness of
spring, it is here.

But rain is not always regenerative. Some of the poet's
most memorable images are of the erosive effects of rain
(without and within) as a reminder of time passing. If
anything accents the sea of eternity—and death—it is the
dripping of the rain, whether it be on our own masked
faces or on "roughly featured stones / With looks eroded
in the rain of time. . . ."[20]

20. From "Sarabande," in *MW*, p. 99; and *NSP*, p. 59.

In "Storm Windows"[21] another reflexive image appears: the frame full of rain crushing the dry grass. Beneath the storm windows lying on the ground (which were not put up because a storm broke) is the grass, streaming "Away in lines like seaweed on the tide / Or blades of wheat leaning against the wind." The dry grass is the green moment, unfulfilled, which, under the glass "Brimful of bouncing water," echoes with a "swaying clarity":

> This lonely afternoon of memories
> And missed desires, while the wintry rain
> (Unspeakable the distance in the mind!)
> Runs on the standing windows and away.

The pane (pain) is separation, which becomes internal in the poem. The grass is the moment, which can only be imagined through the pane (it is only "like" seaweed on the tide—it is not even wet) framed in the mind, as it is in life. The bouncing water, which is also framed, mocks us with time and the lost possibility, echoing what is irretrievably gone.

While rain seems to signify time passing and loneliness, snow has a gentler meaning, but one which is also reflective of time. If rain is erosion, then snow is the moment caught with a perfect singularity. In a lovely short lyric, "Moment" (*NSP*, 3), the opening line is, "Now, starflake frozen on the windowpane . . ." which is an image that, in itself, could be the whole poem—or at least, the type of profile Ezra Pound liked. Snow fascinates Nemerov by its forms ("Runes," VI), which are infinite and never exactly alike. Yet snowflakes, evanescent but enduring in some basic similarity, seem to exemplify the endless possibilities and configurations of nature. Each flake with its perfect and individual symmetry is one of the myriad things in nature

21. In *MW*, p. 8; and *NSP*, p. 41.

which we can never count and never redeem. They are "eccentricities," which make a million designs "to be pleasingly latticed and laced and interfused / And mirrored to the Lord of everything that is by one and one / and one."[22]

In "The View from an Attic Window" (*NSP*, 22–23) the poet tells us that we live in "two kinds of thing":

> The powerful trees, thrusting into the sky
> Their black patience, are one, and that branching
> Relation teaches how we endure and grow;
> The other is the snow,

> Falling in a white chaos from the sky,
> As many as the sands of all the seas,
> As all the men who died or who will die,
> As stars in heaven, as leaves of all the trees. . . .

Snow is both nothingness, in white abstractions, and the everlasting mystery that covers all.

Of the many configurations of water in Nemerov's work, none is more effective than the mountain stream. In the poem "Painting a Mountain Stream"[23] the poet "seeks to set the nature of water in relation to human perception and human imagination."[24] The reflexive image of the stream sets forth the theme of the poem in the first two lines: "Running and standing still at once / is the whole truth"; it is the way in which imagination through perception and reflexion divines the identity and continuity of all paradoxical phenomena.

> . . . Raveled or combed,
> wrinkled or clear, it gets its force
> from losing force. Going it stays.

22. From "Angel and Stone," in *NSP*, pp. 27–29.
23. In *MW*, pp. 97–98; and *NSP*, pp. 57–58.
24. Nemerov, "Attentiveness and Obedience," p. 248.

Pulse beats, and planets echo this,
the running down, the standing still,
all thunder of the one thought.
The mind that thinks it is unfounded.

Here is the reflexive relation between mind and body, mind
and world, seeing and being. In this relation the tensions
of time/eternity, light/darkness, form/substance, ideal/ac-
tual are caught in the balance.

I speak of what is running down.
Of sun, of thunder bearing the rain
I do not speak, of the rising flame
or the slow towering of the elm.

Forces are not to be regarded as static symbols, related by
cause and effect, but measured in the dynamic rhythm of
life, the metamorphic process.

The visible way is always down
but there is no floor to the world.

Study this rhythm, not this thing.
The brush's tip streams from the wrist
of a living man, a dying man.
The running water is the wrist.

The stream (bloodstream) pulses the rhythm of being and
becoming, of living and dying, simultaneously. The visible
way is down, but there is no bottom to the unfathomable
mystery of being. One can only feel its pulse. The running
water (blood), coursing through the rocks (wrist) is the
mystery of the moving force.

In the confluence of the wrist
things and ideas ripple together

as in the clear lake of the eye,
unfathomably, running remains.

In the flow of the stream (bloodstream), the actual and ideal ripple together, reflected in the eye of the mind, where, in the still form, running remains.

The eye travels on running water,
out to the sky, if you let it go.
However often you call it back
it travels again, out to the sky.

Through the eye the world is integrated; but perception, through the light of imagination, is boundless. This is the bringing forth of that which was in darkness.

The water that seemed to stand is gone.
The water that seemed to run is here.
Steady the wrist, steady the eye;
paint this rhythm, not this thing.

Imagination can only mirror visible reality the moment after. The poet seeks to catch the rhythm of life as it happens.

This is one of Nemerov's most charming and musical poems. The reflexive image of stream-life and perception-imagination flows from beginning to end. The tetrameter lines are filled with light, tripping syllables; the rushing movement of the run-on lines is enhanced by the lack of the conventional capitals at the start of each line. Aurally and visually, the poem runs its sparkling course—clear, fresh, and marvelous.

From the poet's use of various water and earth images throughout his work, a unique pattern of symbol and metaphor emerges, giving voice to a vision that is perceptible as the poet's own. He has told us that the world may not be so much a meaning as a rhythm. This thought is conveyed in the many configurations of related earth and water images as they illuminate the poet's constant concern with paradox and metamorphosis. The green ocean, maneuvering in its sleep, suggests the "sleep of causes," the unfathomable dark mystery. The changing face of the sea is that of eternity, forever hidden, but felt through the ebb and flow of the tides. The ocean corresponds to universal experience and, thus, becomes the dominant image in the more philosophical poems, usually in conjunction with rocks, shells, or the shallow soil of civilization. These forms define but are chiefly *defined by* the vast and enduring ocean, for it is the primal force: generative, destructive, and regenerative. It is pure substance, in opposition to form—the dry abstraction, the shapes we give our idolatries, patterned after the hard, rigid solids of earth.

A miniature ocean, the pond too is mysterious and produces myriad forms of life. Yet the pond, unlike the ocean, is temporal, as is man, and has more personal, human associations for the poet: the mystery of birth and death, the dark unconscious (which is also the source of manifold life), and the dark, slimy granules from which the eye is formed and images spring.

The stream is that which, ultimately, links ocean and pond. Fresh water tumbling freely down its course, though directed through the rocks, sings the rhythm of life to the pulsing blood in the veins. The stream becomes the poem— "The clear and mirroring stream / Where images remain although the water / Passes away."[25]

25. From "To Lu Chi," in *MW*, pp. 90–94; and *NSP*, pp. 77–81.

3

FIRE IN THE DIAMOND
DIAMOND IN THE DARK

A RECURRENT THEME in Nemerov's work, especially
in his later poems, is the relation between mind and world,
or the problem of perception and imagination, which marks
the steepest part of the initiatory ascent. The major elements in these poems are light (fire) and space (air).[1]
In these poems Nemerov seeks to illumine the vast spatial
void, within and without, which the mind inhabits. As the
poet has stated, scientific materialism led man to doubt his
traditional concepts of self, mind, and world. Unable to
locate or identify mind in relation to the world, except on a
purely physiological basis, man has barely left the Cartesian
premise of doubt through which, paradoxically, existence is
affirmed: "Cogito ergo sum." In the context of doubt, imagination itself becomes problematic. Concomitant to this situation, as Nemerov suggests in a number of poems, is the
isolation and fragmentation of human experience today,
an outgrowth of an increasingly visual and mechanistic
culture in which one's perspective becomes either telescopic
or microscopic and where the primary human drama is per-

1. "Light" and "space" are preferred here since they are more
applicative words currently than "fire" and "air" and, as such, have
become part of aesthetic, as well as scientific, terminology.

ceived segmentally and secondhand through the visual media. In such a culture, perception is so bombarded and saturated by environmental stimuli that its very nature is lost, and awareness is either deflected or distorted.[2] Literally, nothing is left to (or of) the imagination.

Yet the poet knows that there remain, as always, interior and exterior spaces beyond our ken but not beyond our power to imagine or name. The poetics of space and light is nothing new, for, as Nemerov reminds us, man has most often dealt with reality by its reflection—through the mirror image and the mind imagining. Space is both an inward and outward expansion, the blue void above refracted in the dark abyss behind the eye perceiving.[3] Thus both the classical Psyche myth and Leonardo da Vinci's model of a flying machine have in them a poetry of space and light. In designating invisible areas by such words as "psyche" (the Greek "soul"), or "super ego," "ego," and "id," man has named spatial dimensions beyond the reach of scientific experience.

The association of light (fire) and space (air) with mind, spirit, soul, or a deeper reality has been part of almost all myth systems, particularly in Western civilization. Sir James Frazer records that many primitive peoples

2. One of the many astute analyses of the perceptual problem today is made by Marshall McLuhan and Harley Parker in *Through the Vanishing Point: Space in Poetry and Painting*. Their statement of the problem (page 2) seems to substantiate what Nemerov expresses in the second group of poems in this chapter, namely, that "all the arts might be considered to act as counter-environments or countergradients," and that any environmental form which saturates perception "so that its own character is imperceptible" can "distort or deflect human awareness."

3. This sentence is to be construed in metaphorical terms, although it must necessarily rest on the prevailing view of what determines sight. Reception theories of visual perception replaced emission theories after Newton published his *Optics*. However, the problem of visual perception, as it relates to psychological as well as to physiological processes, is by no means solved and continues to be the subject of much research. One may still question why people perceiving the same object configure it differently, and to what extent conscious or unconscious impulses affect the act of seeing.

believed that a man's soul existed in his shadow or reflection —in water or a mirror. In ancient Greece, as in ancient India, men feared the power of the water spirits, who could drag a person's reflection or soul underwater, leaving him to perish—probably the origin of the Narcissus myth.[4] Certainly, since the highly visual culture of Classical Greece, the mind has been identified with vision and light. Apollo, the sun god, was also the god of reason; the eye was symbolic of the mind. In both Judaism and Christianity, light is a divine attribute; fire frequently manifests some aspect of the divine will. Throughout the Bible, fire and light are associated with the angels and, in the New Testament, with Christ as the Son of God. Among the several hundred scriptural configurations of fire and light are "the flaming sword," "the burning bush," "the lamp" of the law, "tongues of fire," and "the lake of fire."[5]

Similarly, space (or air) has traditionally signified an invisible reality or spirit. The Greek word "pneuma," like the Latin word "spiritus," stood for both spirit and breath; the Greeks, followed by the Romans, personified the winds as the god Aeolus. To the Hebrews, God was "first the breath / That raised a whirlwind in the desert dust. . . ."[6] With Christianity, spirit acquired a more transcendental meaning, symbolized by the dove, but, in the stratified cosmos of the Middle Ages, spirit and soul continued to be associated with air and the celestial realm above and with the equally nebulous regions of the mind. Although man's concepts of space and light changed radically during the Renaissance (and have been changing with greater frequency ever since), many of the earlier myths have retained their meaning, even in an age which has accepted the theories or discoveries of Darwin, Freud, Einstein, Fermi, and Kornberg. Prometheus, Daedalus and Icarus, and Oedi-

4. *The Golden Bough*, p. 192.
5. Cruden's *Complete Concordance* gives more than a hundred examples of the use of fire and light imagery in the Bible.
6. Nemerov, "The View from Pisgah," in *NRD*, p. 30.

pus still speak to our condition. Within the myth complex of our times, the poetry of space and light continues to find articulating possibilities as it redefines the boundaries between the known and the unknown.

Like many contemporary poets, Nemerov has dared to explore those boundaries shifting rapidly in the Scientific Age. Yet he is one of a very few poets to relate art to science and to incorporate scientific phenomena in his work, most notably in those poems about mind and world in which light and space are dominant elements. Yet, in no sense are these poems "period pieces," nor can Nemerov be labeled as a "scientific poet"; even those poems which are most particular and contemporary in reference elucidate his deeper concern for the relation between the visible and the invisible, the concern of poetry through the ages.[7]

While an intensive study of Nemerov's use of scientific imagery is not my objective here, some mention of how he relates art to science may enhance the meaning of the following groups of poems as well as the vision which informs them. As was stated in the Introduction, Nemerov's imagery has an objective honesty about it. The rock on the road is a real rock to the poet and must be perceived as such (with the eye of a naturalist and with all other senses tuned in) before it can be transformed in the mirror of language. The problem of poetry, as Nemerov implies, is to distinguish between what is representational (purely visual) and what is real in relation to all of the senses. In certain respects that is the problem of science, too. Furthermore, the poet recognizes that art and science are alike in that each is experimental, proceeding from hypothesis and under controlled, limiting conditions. However, the aims of art and science, being poles apart, can only be related inversely, which Nemerov illustrates, again using the mirror image: "Art, too, produces its process under controlled

7. This relation, to some extent, is the proper concern of science also, though not for the same reasons.

and limiting conditions, cutting away irrelevancies, speeding up or slowing down the reaction under study, so that the results, whatever they may be, will stand forth with a singular purity and distinction. The instruments of science, of course, have as their aim the creation of an objectivity as nearly as possible universal in character; the poet's aim might be thought of as the same and reversed, a mirror image—to represent in the world the movement of a subjectivity as nearly as possible universal in character" ("The Swaying Form," in *PF*, 15).

In the light of this statement, Nemerov's position as a poet in the Scientific Age is singular, if middle-of-the-road from a philosophical standpoint. Avoiding the two extremes of solipsism and phenomenalism, he is also careful not to misappropriate scientific theory in using it for analogical purposes in his work. His vision, always prismatic, must necessarily reflect scientific knowledge as part of human experience—and, therefore, not alien to poetry—although no one sees with greater irony the impact of science and technology on our lives. Yet he also recognizes that the purpose of the poet and that of the scientist are supplementary—two different ways of the mind to draw nearer to the shadow of an external world.

Among the poems about mind and world, two general types are discernible. The first includes the long philosophical poem or sequence and the short lyric, both of which touch upon the timeless fundamental antithesis: light/darkness, the one/the many, time/eternity, illusion/reality, and ideal/actual. The second type of poem, which is usually satirical or lyrical, conveys contemporary themes: man's sense of unreality or absurdity, alienation, fragmentation; and the simultaneity, relativity, and schizoid aspects of modern life. In both groups of poems, light is defined by darkness and is associated with human consciousness.

We began in wet and darkness, and even into the dry

light we brought that wet and darkness. So much of
what we learned, perhaps the essential forms of all
we ever learn, belong back there, a learning without
understanding that conditions our later understanding . . . of everything.

What is said here of the individual consciousness
may be said also of historical consciousness . . . it
defines itself continuously with the darkness that it is
not, or that it says it is not (*Journal*, 143).

In the first group of poems, natural imagery is used
within a universal context of space and light, for the world
is experienced directly. One of Nemerov's earlier poems,
"Maia" ("Maya"),[8] relates human consciousness to reality,
suggesting the vision that is more fully realized in later
poems. The title is ambiguous but carries the irony implicit
in this short lyric, for Maya is the extraphysical, creative
power in the Vedas—the reality which manifests itself in
the illusory cosmic world. The poem moves backward in
time from civilization's brief moment to the aeons before
it. The first verse presents modern man, the great stone
builder, who, in some ways, has hardly progressed beyond
the Stone Age. The second verse suggests the crossroads of
history, the birth of Christ, and the last two verses return
to the barest simplicities of nature, from which all myths
and images spring.

> Reality! said the stone-minded man
> With his eye on a sky-scraper,
>   This world is hard lines.
>
> Suffer! said the thorny-minded man
> Who sat at the cross-roads,
>   The world is a tangled vine.

8. "Maia" (sometimes interchangeable with "Maya" or "Maja")
has acquired a number of different meanings during the course of
Western civilization. Hence I was delighted to learn from Nemerov

The sun on the streaming water
Imagines rock and branch, the moon
   Imagines the sun,

I die into these images while
The black water and the white
   Water race and remain.

               (*MW,* 83)

Taken as a whole, the poem points to man's illusions of grandeur. What we think we know becomes farther removed in time from the reality of what we are. Like Narcissus, who sees most often his own image in the mirror of nature, we die, unknowing, and return to our watery origins, where life existed long before the evolution of man.

The run-on lines in the last verse are effective, with the final line, "Water race and remain," signifying the whole paradoxical (black and white) truth. On another level, water and sun become images of regeneration, working together: water, as the body substance, rhythm, and source of life; and sun, the mind imagining and making the world intelligible. Light, in this context, as in most of Nemerov's poems, flashes an instant of truth in the void above the dark sea of eternity. In this respect, light is also the mind transcending the limits of body, through imagination, at the moment of convergence when time and eternity cross and the mind becomes one with the world. The connection between mind and sun is that of flame to fire; through this connection the invisible is made visible:

The candle of the sun,
The candle of the mind,

---

that the title of his poem had been misspelled and should be "Maya" (*not* interchangeable with "Maia"), a Sanskrit word which, in Hindu philosophy, is a goddess who personifies illusion.

Twin fires that together
Turn all things inside out.

(*BS*, 85)

The moment of illumination, or of convergence, is
caught in the short poem "Moment" (*NSP*, 3). Here all
paradoxes are resolved and the simultaneity of being and
nonbeing is encompassed, as the mind, from its very depths,
transcends the body and the physical world to lose itself in
the flash across the gap of being, the mind of God.

Now starflake frozen on the windowpane
All of a winter night, the open hearth
Blazing beyond Andromeda, the sea-
Anemone and the downwind seed, O moment
Hastening, halting in a clockwise dust,
The time in all the hospitals is now,
Under the arc-lights where the sentry walks
His lonely wall it never moves from now,
The crying in the cell is also now,
And now is quiet in the tomb as now
Explodes inside the sun, and it is now
In the saddle of space, where argosies of dust
Sail outward blazing, and the mind of God,
The flash across the gap of being, thinks
In the instant absence of forever: now.

Here, Nemerov's aural and visual imagination comes
into play in his characteristic use of enjambment, internal
rhyme, and multivalent images. The meaning of the poem is
enhanced and unified both rhythmically and aurally by the
reiterated "now," like the chime of a bell or a clock, and by
the internal rhyme of such lines as "the sea- / Anemone and
the downwind seed," or "Under the arc-lights where the
sentry walks / His lonely wall. . . ."
    The movement of the lyric is centripetal-centrifugal,

with a secondary up-and-down, or wavelike, motif which
adds to the dynamic effect of the poem. From the circumference of the first two parallel images, the immediate starflake and far-distant star, the lyric moves to encircle two
less separate, but also parallel, images—sea anemone and
downwind seed—then subsides, ever so slightly, in the paradoxical phrase "Hastening, halting in a clockwise dust."
The series of tight, restrictive images in the center of the
poem (hospital, fort, cell, and tomb) gather momentum,
then uncoil in a dynamic thrust into space: "And now is
quiet in the tomb as now / Explodes inside the sun. . . ."

The entire poem is capsuled into a single sentence. The
all-embracing effect, achieved through rhythm and sound, is
greatly enhanced by the repetition of circular images: starflake, open hearth, Andromeda, sea anemone, downwind
seed, clockwise dust, arc-lights, saddle of space, and sun.
The linear or square images (windowpane, lonely wall, cell,
tomb) are temporal, spatially confining figures of separation, yet are resolved in the circularity of the moment. Light
and space are configured in a series of parallel images
which have either a paradoxical or inverse connection when
taken together. All images are multivalent. The "starflake
frozen on the windowpane," signifying light/darkness,
fire/ice, and the beauty of form, is a miniature of the star
named for Andromeda,

> . . . That ill starred Ethiop queen that strove
> To set her beauty's praise above
> The sea-nymphs, and their powers offended.
>
> (Milton, "Il Penseroso," lines 19–21)

The sea anemone, which only superficially resembles a
flower in fórm and color, is paralleled by the downwind
seed, but their relationship is inverse. The sea anemone
reproduces by budding or fission, whereas the seed, com-

pacted full of potential life, is blown by the winds of chance to some far field where it will grow.

The constraining images at the poem's center point to various confining aspects of the body, as opposed to the circular images through which the mind takes flight in the rest of the poem. "Argosies of dust / Sail outward blazing" harks back to "clockwise dust" and to "the open hearth / Blazing beyond Andromeda." The "saddle of space" and "the sun" define each other. Paradox and simultaneity are explicit in the line, "Hastening, halting in a clockwise dust," and are implicit throughout the poem, being most powerfully expressed in the last lines.

The moment of illumination is intuitive—not logical or rational, but a leap of faith made possible by language. Through the paradox of poetic language, the singular act of faith occurs; the many become one, the whole assumes the shape of its various parts. Perhaps the most difficult problem here is the duality of the one and the many, which is the basis of metaphysical poetry, as Nemerov indicates in the following passage: "Now there is, I conceive, one duality that underlies a great deal of poetry, especially the kind . . . that is called . . . 'metaphysical': it is, in largest terms, the duality of the One and the Many. Metaphysical poetry is a poetry of the dilemma, and the dilemma which paradoxes and antitheses continually seek to display is the famous one at which all philosophies falter, the relation of the One with the Many, the leap by which infinity becomes finite, essence becomes existence; the commingling of the spirit with matter, the working of God in the world" ("The Current of the Frozen Stream," in *PF*, 102).

Although mind transcends body, mind is still contiguous with body, for the moment of convergence or illumination is not extracorporeal; spirit is immanent in flesh. Mind, through imagination, transcends bodily limitations but not bodily existence. This rather complex point is clarified by the following excerpt from an essay on Wallace

Stevens in which Nemerov discusses the idea of simultaneity: "The true inheritance, if we are able to see it, is a world already transformed, the lucid realization of one among infinite possibilities of transformation, of projection from the shadowy presence at the center. Concerning this [Stevens] quoted from Whitehead these rather cryptic words: 'In a certain sense, everything is everywhere at all times, for every location involves an aspect of itself in every other location. Thus every spatio-temporal standpoint mirrors the world'" ("The Bread of Faithful Speech," in *PF*, 87).

Both of these passages recall Nemerov's essay on "The Mind's Relation with the World." The duality of mind corresponds to the duality of experience. Subjectivity must necessarily be dual, for through the self-reflexiveness of doubt existence is affirmed. The response of mind to world is always double though it may also be total. Beauty, truth, virtue may only be defined in paradoxical terms, for they are not understood as nouns but as states of being.

Beauty, always closely associated with mortality, is the shadow of the moment realized and the illumination of the stillness that is not. In "Maiden with Orb and Planets" (*NRD*, 31), beauty is pictured as "shy among the destinies, / Daughter and mother of the silent crossings." Beauty is "the petaled time / In a child's tomb, the basalt time that waits / In the Valley of the Kings. . . ." Beauty is also, paradoxically, "the swaying time / That smoothes the rivers through the summer nights / And polishes the stone and dulls the eye." Our awareness of mortality is what illuminates the moment of life and makes it beautiful—and hopeless.

> Her stillness makes the moment of the world
> Strike once, and that is what beauty is,
> To stand as Agamemnon's daughter stood
> Amid great armies waiting on the wind.

Beauty is poised always between life and death, while imagination waits in the wings to catch her as she falls.

The problem of imagination—the limitation of art as a mirror held up to nature—is explored from different perspectives in many of Nemerov's poems. His later work shows a greater acceptance of the limits of art and a deeper appreciation of life, even of illusion. Many of the poems in *The Blue Swallows* reveal a fascination with the effects of light on familiar, material objects. These poems are suffused with sunlight and shadow, flame, firelight, and warmth.

By contrast, in his earlier poems light is often used in an unrealistic, eerie manner, suggesting the poet's despair and sense of detachment. The following sonnet, titled "The Sunglasses" (*MW*, 7), is placed here, rather than with the contemporary poems, because its mood is one that all poets have suffered at one time or another: the terrible ennui and depression that come when inspiration is gone and life, as well as art, seems a cruel joke. Many a poet has felt enslaved by a Muse who might be Circe, Acrasia, the Lorelei, or La Belle Dame sans Merci.

> The terrible temper of the day gone dim
> Against this lucid calm, the green lagoon
> That turns my drowning eyes to precious stone,
> I stare unpunished at the sun's wild limb
> Of Satan wavering westward past the noon
> In a mild fire, foolish gold; whose trim
> Of wicked brilliance not the seraphim
> Could hold a candle to, or light a moon.
>
> Against my glass, all light is pacified
> Here where I lie in green gone deeper green,
> All colors colder; I, dreaming I died
> Where in still waters on illusion's coast
> The cold-eyed sirens sang to sailor men
> Of jewels that charred the zenith, and were lost.

The reflexive image, eye-vision, is configured in cold
colors and hard objects throughout the poem. Vision is ob-
structed by the tinged glasses that separate the poet from
the true colors of the landscape. "The green lagoon / That
turns my drowning eyes to precious stone" becomes the
"still waters on illusions's coast" where "The cold-eyed
sirens sang to sailor men / Of jewels that charred the
zenith, and were lost."

The terrible heat of the day is dimmed, for the time
is late afternoon. The lagoon is revealed in a weird light,
while the sun is a "mild fire, foolish gold"—a cold color
which is not the true light of the sun that the moon reflects.
The moon here is, perhaps, the White Goddess or a more
constant Muse. (The Muse conceived of as the White Goddess
is the subject of a book by Robert Graves.)[9] Separated by
the strange green glass of his own vision, paralleling the
green lagoon, the poet is lost in illusion and unable to see
even the reflection of reality.

In another poem, "Holding the Mirror up to Nature,"[10]
the same desperate attitude toward the lack of meaning in
things is evident, though expressed with greater irony:

Some shapes cannot be seen in a glass,
those are the ones the heart breaks at.
They will never become valentines
or crucifixes, never. . . .

"Night clouds / go on insanely as themselves," though, as
the poet tells us, "metaphors would be prettier. . . ." When
he sees those clouds "massed at the edge / of the globe, neither weasel nor whale," he wonders if the world is non-
representational, after all. Suddenly the unspeakable truth
breaks upon him.

9. *The White Goddess* (New York: Vintage Books, 1958).
10. In *MW*, p. 102; *NSP*, p. 60.

> . . . I know
> a truth that cannot be told, although
> I try to tell you, "We are alone,
> we know nothing, nothing, we shall die
> frightened in our freedom, the one
> who survives will change his name
> to evade the vengeance for love. . . ."
> Meanwhile the clouds go on clowning
> over our heads in the floodlight of
> a moon who is known to be Artemis
> and Cynthia but sails away anyhow
> beyond the serious poets with their
> crazy ladies and cloudy histories,
> their heroes in whose idiot dreams
> the buzzard circles like a clock.

The poem is almost a parody of mind and imagination. Life is either meaningless or incomprehensible, for the truth is that we are alone in space and time. A similar feeling is grasped in the epigram "Invocation" (*MW*, 62), which addresses the wasp, reminiscent of "the gad-fly of Athens," Socrates the wise—the stinger of souls searching for truth and virtue.

> Wasp, climbing the window pane
> And falling back on the sill—
> What buzz in the brain
> And tremor of the will,
> What climbing anger you excite
> Where my images brim and spill
> In failures of the full light.

Falling into the same mood, the poet is able to transcend it in "The Loon's Cry" (*MW*, 29–32). The time, in this long poem, is a cold evening at the end of summer as the sun goes down and the moon rises. In the red sun and

white moon the poet sees natural beauty, not theology, for
he says that he has "fallen from / The symboled world,
where I in earlier days / Found mysteries of meaning, form
and fate / Signed on the sky. . . ." In those days he stood
between "A swamp fire and a reflecting rock." He recalls
how he once envied those past ages when energy shone
through things:

> Under the austere power of the scene
> The moon standing balanced against the sun,
> I simplified still more, and thought that now
> We'd traded all those mysteries in for things,
> For essences in things, not understood—
> Reality in things! And now we saw
> Reality exhausted all their truth.

As if in answer to the poet's thought, a loon cries out,
"Laughter of desolation on the river, / A savage cry. . . ."
Again the loon cries out, but, this time, his voice is "emptied of that sense / Or any other" and the poet becomes
like Adam, "Hearing the first loon cry in paradise," in a
blessed state of ignorance. To the poet, that cry signifies
the loon's contempt for the form of things, the "doctrines,
which decayed—the nouns of stone / And adjectives of
glass—not for the verb. . . ." The verb is not static; it is
"being" which surges eternally "Against the sea wall of the
solid world. . . ." The poet's act is the "respeaking" of the
verb:

> Only and always, in whatever time
> Stripped by uncertainty, despair and ruin,
> Time readying to die, unable to die
> But damned to life again, and the loon's cry.

Meditating that the moon might have been such a world
as ours until it went cold inside (since no amount of sun

can keep people "Warm in their palaces of glass and stone"),
the poet wonders about the stars, too—whether they were
once worlds—and recognition dawns that there *are* signatures in all things which may be found and named again
through art. In the final verse a train whistles in the darkness. The sound echoes the lost cry of the loon to the mind
believing in nature's inscription on all things—not in
"nouns of stone" or "adjectives of glass," but in the mystery of the verb, "being."

The problem of subjectivity in isolation is a constant
theme with Nemerov. "Idea" (*NRD*, 23) conveys the singularity, emptiness, and absurdity of abstract thought.
"Idea blazes in darkness, a lonely star," for "the witching
hour is not twelve but one." A fine line separates pure principle from madness, yet "the independent mind thinks on, /
Breathing and burning, abstract as air." The poet compares
abstract thought to a game of chess in which one learns
"to do without the pieces first, / And then the board; and
finally, I guess, / Without the game." (The absurdity of the
situation, as well as the figures of chessboard and lightship,
suggest the basic imagery pattern in Samuel Beckett's one-
act play *Endgame*.) Suddenly this lightship is unmoored
and goes adrift, "Endangering others with its own dis-
tress." But, as long as light remains, man will chart the
world in his merry, mad, adventurous way:

> O holy light! All other stars are gone,
> The shapeless constellations sag and fall
> Till navigation fails, though ships go on
> This merry, mad adventure as before
> Their single-minded masters meant to drown.

Thought, or reflexion, is like the "celestial globe"—
"the world / Without the world." One may hold it in the
hand, "A hollow sphere of childlike blue / With magnitudes
of stars."

There in its utter dark
The singing planets go,
And the sun, great source,
Is blazing forth his fires
Over the many-oceaned
And river-shining earth
Whereon I stand
Balancing this ball
Upon my hand.

> ("Celestial Globe,"
> in *BS*, 84–85)

Like "the universe, / The turning One," reflection turns on itself, separate but microcosmic. Speculation is "the world / Beyond the World," which one may wear on the head "As a candle wears a pumpkin / At Halloween, when children / Rise as the dead. . . ." Imagination is an inversion of reality; the candle of the sun and the candle of the mind turn all things inside out.[11]

Most of the poems in Part IV of *The Blue Swallows* are infused with light, creating patterns from spatial objects. In the very beautiful title poem (89–90), space and light combine with water as dominant elements. The poet, standing on a bridge across the millstream, looks down below and sees

Seven blue swallows divide the air
In shapes invisible and evanescent,

11. Referring to this poem in a personal letter (June 22, 1969) Nemerov says: "If you try to find accurate figures for the situation of someone looking at a celestial globe (I borrowed one from the Library of Congress Map Division and kept it on my desk all the time I was there), you see how odd and hard it is to do, for what you are looking at is an inside-out arrangement of what figuratively you—and the earth, and the sun—are inside. The pumpkin figure may remotely be a reminiscence of Blake in *Milton* (I, 31) in the beautiful passage about space beginning 'The sky is an immortal Tent built by the Sons of Los,' where you could express his intention by saying that each of us wears the horizon for his hatbrim."

Kaleidoscopic beyond the mind's
Or memory's power to keep them there.

The mind, helplessly, "Weaves up relation's spindrift web, /
Seeing the swallows' tails as nibs / Dipped in invisible ink,
writing . . ." but the poet is reminded that it is he who is
ascribing God's or nature's authorship to the birds and
seeing their inscriptions on the air:

> . . . Ah, poor ghost,
> You've capitalized your Self enough.
> That villainous William of Occam
> Cut out the feet from under that dream
> Some seven centuries ago.

It has taken all that time for us to see with "opened eyes
emptied of speech / The real world where the spelling mind"

> Imposes with its grammar book
> Unreal relations on the blue
> Swallows.

The poet reflects the truth awakened in him—that

> even the water
> Flowing away beneath those birds
> Will fail to reflect their flying forms,
> And the eyes that see become as stones
> Whence never tears shall fall again.

The swallows correspond to the poet's thoughts, creating meaning and relation out of the invisible air. A passage
in which Nemerov speaks of Wallace Stevens' pigeons
serves to illumine this aspect of the swallows, for they,
too, are "as thoughts, or as the manner of our perceiving
thoughts between the bright emptiness above and the gen-

erative dark beneath, mediators which without solving re-
solve."[12] The moment passes with the lost shadow of bird
wings on water, yet the swallows remain in the mind, as
does the echo of the poet's words:

> O swallows, swallows, poems are not
> The point. Finding again the world,
> That is the point, where loveliness
> Adorns intelligible things
> Because the mind's eye lit the sun.

Nemerov's fascination with the play of light on familiar objects is evident in "Firelight in Sunlight" (*BS*, 104)
and "Interiors" (*BS*, 105). In both poems, illumination and
renewal are associated. "Firelight in Sunlight" abounds
with joy in the simple details of daily life. The regenerative
power of light is made synonymous with the creative, purgative force of water in the following image:

> Firelight in sunlight, silver-pale
> Streaming with emerald, copper, sapphire
> Ribbons and rivers, banners, fountains;
> They rise, they run swiftly away.

The flow of water figures, emerging from the shapes and
colors of firelight in sunlight, is illusory but no less real
to the poet, for these are his "mysteries to see / And say
and celebrate with words / In orders until now reserved."
With a new wonder he perceives how

> apple logs unlock their sunlight
> In the many-windowed room to meet
> New sunlight falling in silvered gold
> Through the fern-ice forest of the glass. . . .

12. "The Bread of Faithful Speech," in *PF*, p. 88.

How striking the texture in this poem—the feeling of warmth in contrast to cold in "the fern-ice forest of the glass." The world becomes an "early world" to the poet as he sees the "pulsing constancies of flame / Warping a form along the log's / Slowly disintegrating face / Crackled and etched, so quickly aged. . . ." A new voice is heard: the mellow tones of middle age perhaps, when contentment is found in small things and within the spaces where one lives. Through imagery of light and space, the poet sings out some inward discovery of his own.

> For light is in the language now,
> Carbon and sullen diamond break
> Out of the glossary of earth
> In holy signs and scintillations,
> Release their fiery emblems to
> Renewal's room and morning's room
> Where sun and fire once again
> Phase in the figure of the dance
> From far beginnings here returned,
> Leapt from the maze at the forest's heart,
> O moment where the lost is found!

The sequel to "Firelight in Sunlight" is "Interiors"— a miniature Song of Solomon in that it can be read as either a religious or a love poem but reads most effectively as both. However, "Interiors" is more like a tapestry than a song, which may account for some of the problems of interpretation. What the poet attempts to do, seemingly, is to fuse all the nuances of the love/death and resurrection theme into a single expression which is, at once, spiritual and physical, universal and deeply personal.

The poem is structured on the ancient (and nearly universal) ritual in which the king was sacrificed when his strength failed, or after a fixed term of years. In later times, the king could substitute his son in the sacrifice, since he, too, was invested with divine attributes.[13] While the original meaning, or meanings, of these primitive rites remain anthropological questions, the archetypal ritualistic pattern is repeated, with minor variations, in the Adonis myths, the story of Abraham and Isaac, the Passion of Christ, and the vegetation rites (such as the "ceremony called Burning of Wands," mentioned here in line 10) which prevailed throughout most of Europe during the Middle Ages. The broad range of this pattern, in its pagan and Christian manifestations, is inferred through the symbols and figures in the poem, many of which have phallic significance as well.

Within the fabric of the poem, the images form a spatial design which is discontinuous in a linear way but has the repetitive and multilevel aspects of a medieval tapestry or allegory. For example, the peripheral images in the first four lines are repeated, narrowed visually (to the point where they become merged), and intensified emotionally in the last stanza (lines 15–22), as consciousness leaves the exterior world of objects in the castle and courtyard and becomes lost in the deep interiors of the self, beyond the shadows of the mirror of mind which reflects the unconscious and, also, a universal unconscious.

Radiating from the center of these spatial patterns is the unifying and reflexive image of the "small flame," which begins and ends the poem. While the relationship between mind and body, or spirit and flesh, has often been analogized as a house or castle, the title and basic image of this poem suggest *El Castille Interior y Morades* (The Interior Castle) of St. Teresa of Ávila. "The small flame" corresponds to the divine spark which Teresa experienced in the fourth mansion of the castle as she came nearer to the Divine Presence. The outer courtyard in the opening stanza is dark and cold like Teresa's, which is infested by toads and other abominable creatures.[14] The poem, like the

13. Frazer, *The Golden Bough*, pp. 264–93.
14. John Beevers, *St. Teresa of Ávila*, pp. 143–44.

story, moves from the outer circumference of the castle to its center.

The problem, as well as the success, of the poem derives not so much from its basic design as from the complex diverse threads woven into it. The poet has appropriated a number of figures and metaphors from myth and legend, all of which pertain to the fertility rites or to sacrifice; yet most of these figures are removed from their traditional contexts and used in a highly unconventional, original way. Since the poem is infused with multilevel meanings and has the logic of a dream or stream of consciousness, these symbolic figures are all the more intriguing and effective when juxtaposed in the context of the poem, where their significance is particular as well as universal.

The flame, in the opening lines, is not only identified with consciousness, or mind, but also with the body, for the objects illuminated are sensuous and phallic as well as regal. "God of battles" (line 3) is probably a direct reference to Ares (Mars), who is emblematic of all that is dominantly male and who was Aphrodite's lover. Originally, Ares was a god of fertility, as well as the god of war, which makes his presence here more credible. In lines 3–10, the flame is associated with sacrifice: first, in the burning of animal flesh to the god of war; and, second, in the vegetation rites, the ceremony of the Burning of Wands. "The hooded women" carrying "uprooted canes" remain somewhat shrouded in mystery, although we know they performed some function in this type of ritual. The "uprooted canes" are obviously phallic symbols of fertility. Not to be discounted here, by inference, is the Knight of the Wands of Tarot deck legend. Although little is known about his prototype, he presumably was the sacrificial knight in the fertility rites, either literally or figuratively. According to Tarot legend, this knight symbolizes flight or departure, or an advancement into the unknown, which meanings are hinted at in the following stanza.

The second stanza is somewhat ambiguous and contains an element of foreboding as well as anticipation that something momentous will happen. Death is suggested indirectly by the traditional symbol of the rider on horseback, yet his tidings are "Peremptory, urgently magnificent," and there is the sense that the ultimatum of death carries also the promise of resurrection.

In the last stanza, the sacrifice is culminated in the act of love when spirit and flesh become one. All of the earlier images are merged here into a singular meaning. Both the Old and New Testaments are echoed in "the book of the body . . . / Where the spirit and the bride say, Come. . . ." The last lines recall Genesis, that man was made in God's image. God's first act was Creation, His first words, "Let there be light" (Genesis 1:3). The small flame of human consciousness becomes the secret of creation, the image or spark of the divine light of the Creator:

> So warm, so clear at the line of corded velvet
> The marvelous flesh, its faster rise and fall,
> Sigh in the throat, the mouth fallen open,
> The knees fallen open, the heavy flag of the skirt
> Urgently gathered together, quick, so quick,
> Black lacquer, bronze, blue velvet, gleam
> Of pewter in a tarnishing light, the book
> Of the body lying open at the last leaf,
> Where the spirit and the bride say, Come,
> As from deep mirrors on the hinted wall
> Beyond these shadows, a small flame sprouts.

The sense of fulfillment, so pronounced in Nemerov's later work, is missing in the second group of poems which deal with contemporary themes. In this group, space is often confining or limited by mirrors, windows, the movie or television screen, and the camera's lens, for the world is perceived indirectly in a fragmentary way. Light is frequently produced by mechanical or artificial means; its effect is one of duplicity and illusion. These poems display loneliness, frustration, and hopelessness, all of which are part of the modern syndrome. The poet is either split internally or against the world, or expresses the divisive situations in life around him.

Characteristic of this group is "The Mirror" (*MW*, 3). In this brief lyric, the poet looks into the glass which separates him from the world and sees his other, or separate, self. The mirror is a "room of silences," an "alien land / Where likeness lies" which is as mysterious as the other (physical) world reflected behind him: "the branch, the same leaf curled / Against the branch," are "quivering duplicities / Rendered again under a distant light." The poet is a stranger to himself and to the world.

> Now slowly the snow drifts down, and coming night
> Darkens the room, while in the leaden glass
> I watch with observed eyes the stranger pass.

The schizoid aspect of reflexivity and of modern life is the subject of "Endegeeste, Anecdote after Ortega y Gasset" (*MW*, 77). Endegeeste, once the home of Descartes, is now an insane asylum. Among the lengthening shadows on the lawn, where Descartes described "the modern thought," "the mindless" come and go. Life is frightening today, as it was in Descartes' time. The identification of two reflexive minds is unmistakable.

> I live in a great and terrifying time,
> As Descartes did. For both of us the dream
> Has turned like milk, and the straight, slender tree
> Twisted at root and branch hysterically.
>
> I keep my reasonable doubt as gay
> As any—though on the lawn they seem to say,
> Those patient, nodding heads, "sum, ergo sum."
> The elm's long shadows fall cold in my room.

The reality of our times, which so often comes to us secondhand via the television screen, movies, or car radio, takes on the quality of absurdity: the newsreel shows the bloody battlefield as we sit munching popcorn; drinking scotch-on-the-rocks, we watch the computer predict who will become president of these United States—tomorrow. Because of the speed of communication and technological invention, reality is, paradoxically, nearer and farther than before, more available to our eyes and ears but more remote from experience, for we only see and hear a fragment of that reality. It becomes like "a play within a play, a picture within a picture." Bombarded on all sides by bits of experience, man's power of reflexion is driven constantly inward, unless he becomes completely outer-directed. For the thinker, escape is impossible in an automated society. The only chance for autonomy is to abstract oneself from the times, yet this recourse, also, is doomed to absurdity or madness. Such is the mood of "Orphic Scenario, For a Movie of Hamlet" (MW, 50–52), which begins as follows:

> . . . Reality
> Comes dearer, but reality's much the same
> As this dark malodorous box of taken tricks,
> Reality's where the hurled light beams and breaks,
> Against the solemn wall, a spattered egg,
> The seed and food of being. If the seed
> And food, split open thus, splayed as a blaze
> On the blank of limit, focused on the yolk
> Or might-be-meat of things, should still entrance
> The vacant stare, fix it with visions of,
> However dripping and impure, an order,
> That is enough, or the abstract of enough.

Order, the poet continues, is made of such refuse, for "eternity / Lusts after the productions of time." Let fastidious Prince Hamlet consider that after all, "It is a play / Within a play, a mystery of infinite / Reflexions. . . ."

Never since Plato's cave has there been a "meatier" or
"more meet" "catch-all for the conscience."

>   . . . Let each man pay
> His own admission: his prismatic self
> Will break the Godhead into comedy.
> He will be purged, order will be restored,
> And he may hear something to his advantage,
> Viewing. . . .

The egg, which is a reflexive image, is a traditional
symbol for creation, being, or the seat of the soul. Many
ancient countries which traded with the Phoenicians
adopted their belief that the world sprang from the egg of
a Creator. Thus, mythology substantiates the well-worn
question "which came first, the chicken or the egg?" The
egg, here, is identified with reality. From the splattered
yolk on the movie screen, the egg image becomes that of
the Phoenix:

>   . . . The great bird of light,
> Phoenix of Araby, splayed on the dark,
> Its planes of cleavage, rhythms of its growth
> Rudely abrupted for the sakes of us
> The understanders. Its violated yolk
> Will shadow forth the form and pressure of
> The body of the age, its shadows move
> Us, shadow-man come forth of shadow-woman,
> Shedding their light without our heat, their sweetness
> Cast accidentally from corrupted substance.
> This moment of the close-up and the clinch
> Desire sighs, prudence makes up its mind,
> While terror moistens on the shining lips
> And the dry tips of hair gigantically
> Shake and are swayed: Our stars have fire hearts.

The artificial scene on the movie screen parallels the real

one and the shadow forms in which we exist, like the Phoenix—neither man nor woman. But deeper reflection and introspection is no answer. In the following lines the poet bends the egg image with true wit and irony. In these lines, the mad Ophelia's voice is heard—lilting, detached, yet strangely rational in a schizophrenic world—followed by the more sober tones of Horatio:

> Priestess and priest display
> The new Veronica, the stiffened face,
> Light of the world, cast on a hanging cloth,
> The egghead's Rorschach in the Holy Wood.
> Minos is dead and Pharoah buried.
> All gone where the green grass goes winters.
> This way to the Egress,
>
> And see, sweet prince,
> How all the buildings rise in a colder sky,
> Cheaper, and yet more golden, than before,
> More high and solemn, borne on a great stage
> In a failing light. . . .
>
> (*MW*, 51–52)

The play on the name "Veronica" is especially apropos to this scene. One recalls the legendary St. Veronica, the woman of Jerusalem who wiped Christ's bleeding face with her veil on the road to Calvary. The image of His face was said to have appeared, miraculously, on her veil; hence, a veronica has come to mean the image of Christ's face imprinted on a handkerchief or cloth. "The new Veronica," also an image, refers to Veronica Lake, who, at the time this poem was written, was idolized as a stage and screen star. Photographed, usually in a stereotyped pose, with her long platinum hair draped seductively over one eye, Veronica Lake endured the private misfortunes, as well as the acclaim, of epitomizing sex and glamour, very briefly, to a fickle public, and of having her image shaped and exploited

by producers, directors, and publicity agents, to further
their own ends. However, the essential equation here is
that the image of the movie star, or idol, is cast on the
screen as the image of Jesus was imprinted on Veronica's
cloth.

Thus the mad world reflected, here, is one in which the
kings and priests of Hollywood and the media—the public
image-makers—reign supreme. Production is more mam-
moth and relatively cheaper than ever before, but the great
stage of the world rises in a failing light, and the kings,
too, will go the way of Minos and Pharoah. The sun's
energy is slowly diminishing, and man has so far failed to
solve the problem of life through the light of reason; we
reproduce existence in the artificial light of the camera
and movie screen. Reflexion is looking backwards, not being
or becoming. Looking back was fatal for both Orpheus and
Hamlet. Likewise, for the reflexive man today existence is
a cold product—a play within a play, or a "dark malodorous
box of taken tricks." Reality, if one must think about it, is
the egg of the Phoenix, that bird which is immortal, con-
suming itself every five or six hundred years and rising
again from its own ashes to shadow forth "the forms and
pressures of the body of the age."

The mood of "Orphic Scenario, For a Movie of Hamlet," is also caught in "The Human Condition" (*BS*, 18),
where the poet portrays the emptiness and fragmentation
of the boxes in which we live. The reflexive image in this
poem is the "picture within a picture" or the "frame within
a frame." Space, projected outwardly in a succession of
boxed or framed figures, becomes progressively confined and
confining, corresponding to the poet's inner sense of desolation and imprisonment. As the poem opens, he is in a
motel room (a box) where he "was told to wait," looking at
the television screen which stands before a picture window.

> . . . Nothing could be more
> Use to a man than knowing where he's at,

And I don't know, but pace the day in doubt
Between my looking in and looking out.

The second stanza depicts the snowy scene and cars
passing outside behind the television screen, where "heads
of heroes can be seen / And sometimes cars, that speed
across the glass." These parallel images seem to suggest to
the poet a time when he once saw "world and thought
exactly meet" in a picture by Magritte, which was actually

A picture of a picture, by Magritte,
Wherein a landscape on an easel stands
Before a window opening on a land-
scape, and the pair of them a perfect fit,
Silent and mad. You know right off, the room
Before that scene was always an empty room.

That is the room in which the poet now stands waiting,
restlessly, as darkness comes, while the TV keeps on going
and "headlights blaze behind / Its legendary traffic, love
and hate, / In this motel where I was told to wait." In
reading this poem, one is reminded of those "nests of boxes"
which children play with in fascination. Here, however,
there is no delight, no pleasure in fitting the parts together,
for the image is an inverse, empty one, progressing inward
toward silence and madness.

Spatial expansion has its outward as well as internal
limits. Man continues to explore the unknown through the
field of science. "Limits" (*MW*, 88) is a poem about man's
eternal, and sometimes fatal, search for knowledge against
impossible odds. The frogmen, seeking the scholarly truth
in the cypress swamps, are striving against such odds:

Leaching the whole of truth,
Ruined heroes of the daily mind,
Those undergoing scholars climb upstream
Into a darkness prior to their dream,
Where the dividing eye is blind.

Inside the "pouched, hard hide of the riddled earth," these
determined frogmen "flutter," ready

> To carry air and light
> Into the condemned, tight
> Tenements of the old landlady
> Till she have rent them more than bed and birth.

In spite of such idealistic motives, the air goes and the
battery burns out. "Is there a second," the poet asks, "of
a second freedom greater than the first," before the lungs
burst? Does the young frog prince, "born of doubt," ever
swim down upon his bride? Does man ever "know" truth,
in the biblical sense of that word?

Yet truth drags man to her, like a mirror, although
to see her face-to-face has dire consequences: Oedipus blinding himself, Narcissus dying of love for his own image.
The sad irony and paradox of man's valiant strivings is
compressed into the last lines:

> All that was lost, they fall to find
> Losing their science, which is understood.

The limits of vision, of both eye and mind, are implied
in poems where mirrors, windows, or pictures are figured.
These images, also, may signify separation or the aborted
hope. All of these meanings are expressed in "De Anima"
(NRD, 25), a poem concerned with the great divisions
between us in spite of proximity.

In the first verse of the poem, a girl stands at a
window in a brilliantly lit room, looking out in the framed
darkness and seeing only her own image. In the following
verse, a young man, across the street in an unlit room, sees
the girl. "They might be in love, might be about to meet, /
If this were a romance," the poet says. In looking at herself,
the girl "tries to look / Beyond herself, and half become

another," trying to see herself, perhaps, as a lover might see her. The other, the potential lover, looks into her crystalline room, seeing her clearly and hopelessly desiring a life that is not his.

> Given the blindness of her self-possession,
> The luminous vision revealed to his despair,
> We look to both sides of the glass at once
> And see no future in it.

Recognizing that "These pure divisions hurt us in some realm / Of parable beyond belief," and "beyond / The temporal mind," the poet asks why it is sorrowful—why we want them together. "Is it the spirit, ransacking through the earth / After its image, its being, its begetting?" The spirit sorrows because lovers bring death into the world. As the poet remarks, this is the type of romance "that lords and ladies listen to / With selfish tears, when she draws down the shade, / When he has turned away" and when

> the blind embryo with his bow of bees,
> His candied arrows, tipped with flower heads,
> Turns from them too, for mercy or for grief
> Refusing to be, refusing to die.

Bees, like wasps, are stinging symbols of the true fact. In this poem love, like beauty, is associated with death. It is an old situation, but the reflexive image—of the dark window of the brilliant room where the girl stands, seeing her own face, and the dark room from which the boy sees the girl—synthesizes the separation, the despair, and inability to communicate, in spite of proximity, that characterize life today.

The relativity and illusion of experience in space and time are captured in "The Junction on a Warm Afternoon" (*NRD*, 34). The poignancy of time passing is caught in a

moment familiar to those who have grown up in the age of
railroads, which are already disappearing:

> . . . The old railroad men
> Are growing obsolete with the great
> Engines whose demands they meet,
> And yet they do not fail in their
> Courtly consideration of the stranger
> Standing in sunlight. . . .

The freight train slowly passes, disappearing among small
trees and "Leaving empty the long, shining rails / That
curve, divide, vanish and remain." The illusion of the shining rails, as seen from the back of a train, reflects the
linear truth of our experience in space and time.

Reality and illusion, the meaning or the lack of meaning in life, are touched upon in "These Words Also" (*NRD*,
36), which tells of a young girl's suicide. The moment of
life in time becomes magnified, especially when death comes
prematurely and is self-inflicted. The shock and unreality
of the discovery parallels the lost life and its disillusion-
ment; both are conveyed through the hard brilliance of
natural and artificial imagery.

> The garden holds its sunlight heavy and still
> As if in a gold frame around the flowers
> That nod and never change, the picture-book
> Flowers of someone's forbidden childhood,
> Pale lemony lilies, pansies with brilliant scowls
> Pretending to be children. Only they live,
> And it is beautiful enough, to live,
> Having to do with hunger and reflection,
> A matter of thresholds, of thoughtless balancings.

Those lines are weighted with shock in the disparity
between the bright morning and the fact of death. The

strange sunlit garden, locked as if in a gold frame, holds
the indelible image of the sensitive flower, forced prematurely into perfect bloom and death. The moment of life
seems infinitely precious when such things happen, yet,
being human, we identify with the other and try to justify
the act in larger terms, perhaps, to solace our own grief.
The poet's response is most human: "The black and gold
morning goes on, and / What is a girl's life?" In the last
image of the poem, life seems as relevant or as purposeful
as the ant's, against the backdrop of eternity.

> . . . There on the path
> Red ants are pulling a shiny beetle along
> Through the toy kingdom where nobody thinks.

Form without essence, existence perceived secondhand,
are symbolized by the picture book, the graven image, and
the photograph. In *Journal of the Fictive Life*, Nemerov
has a good deal to say about photography, which represents
the type of "natural image" that poetry must avoid: "People, tourists, say, who habitually respond to a sight by
photographing it, appear to me very defensive about life.
As though they wished to kill reality in order to guarantee
it, as though only the two-dimensional past were to have a
real (a historical) existence. They are ever-present wit-
nesses to the character of civilization as mediate, abstract,
in a sense *memorized*; the living memory delegated to that
'objective' one in the black box" (81). The poet adds that
the camera's initial lie is the phrase "the camera cannot lie"
and, also, a similar phrase, "One picture is worth a thousand words." The camera, a product of a materialistic civilization, only reports the surface of things "in simple location in time and space" (Whitehead): "Language, on the
contrary, asserts reality to be secret, invisible, a product of
relations rather than things. The camera, whether in the
hands of a reporter or scientist or detective, pries into

secrets, wants everything 'exposed' and 'developed.' . . . The camera wants to 'know.' But if my hypothesis is correct, this knowledge is dialectically determined to be unsatisfying, so that there can be no end to taking pictures. . . . Everything known becomes an object, unsatisfactory . . . hence to be treated with contempt and forgotten in the illusory thrill of taking the next picture" (*Journal*, 82).

The poet cites "The View from Pisgah" (*NRD*, 30) as an example of what tourists photograph. Like the Vatican, Sphinx, or the Badlands, such a scene is associated with authority, mystery, and sterility. In the opening lines, the poet states that

> Our God was to be a breath, and not a postcard
> Of the sun setting over Niagara Falls
> "Wish you were here."

Our God, Who was "first the breath / That raised a whirlwind in the desert dust, / The Wilderness of Sin," became a word "Unspeakable" and, then, a "stillness" and "a standing stone / Set in the road." All is dry; there is "Nothing but sky and sand / to purify a forbidden generation / Of Egypt's kitchens." The photograph portrays the same arid wilderness the poet has wandered in for forty years,

> Lifting mirages to break horizons, dreaming
> Idolatries to alphabet the void,
> Sending those postcards to the Self at home:
> Sunlight on pouring water; wish I were here.

The camera, as it is commonly used, does not create; it merely records the shapes of things. One recalls Sherrington's distinction between eye and camera: the adjustment of the lens of the camera to more or less light is made by the observer working the instrument but, in the eye, that adjustment is automatic, worked by the image itself!

The correspondence between the external and internal image is part of the method, as well as the pattern, in "The Scales of the Eyes," a complex poem sequence which defies classification yet foreshadows the vision of the later sequence "Runes." In "The Scales of the Eyes," the elemental ascent can be traced in both form and imagery. Composed during the same period as "The Salt Garden," the sequence may also be read on three levels although it is, primarily, an introspective poem—an argosy to the center or essence of Self.

Nemerov acknowledges the perceptive explication of this sequence by his friend Kenneth Burke.[15] Burke, without consulting Nemerov,[16] has made observations which provide useful clues to Nemerov's work and are especially helpful in unravelling the intricacies of this poem sequence. Burke regards these poems as a literary species, "best analyzable as radiations from a single center, rather than an over-all development. . . . Otherwise put: the poems are related to one another as moments of a single motive (properties of a single essence)."[17] He summarizes the contents of the poems as "Typical Moments of the Poetizing Self in Motive."[18] In these poems the poet seeks the essence of himself, and, as in "The Salt Garden," that search is in terms of his vocation.

The title "The Scales of the Eyes," an allusion to Acts 9:18, suggests that the quest of the argosy will be revelational, accompanied by a state of vision/blindness. (The biblical passage describes the scales dropping from Paul's eyes as his sight returns after the three-day period of blindness, which began when his "eyes were opened" on the road to Damascus.) In the opening quatrain, the argosy theme, with its predatory and subjective aspects, is estab-

15. Personal letter, October 9, 1968.
16. Ibid.
17. "Comments on Eighteen Poems by Howard Nemerov," p. 130.
18. Ibid., p. 129.

lished through the reflexion and inversion of the first image,
"To fleece the Fleece. . . ." (The argosy, as Burke states, has
predatory and acquisitive overtones, but is also introspective. He describes it as "a journey-to-the-center," or "to the
farthest circumference," where the poet "will seek a definition of his essence in terms of mythic beginnings," using
nature "not naturalistically, but mythically.")[19] The primary image, despite its apparent simplicity, is very complex. Working on at least three levels of meaning, it is a
natural image with both mythic and mundane associations.
More importantly, it poses the question (the quest) of the
argosy: what am I, a thinking creature, in relation to the
universe?

> To fleece the Fleece from golden sheep
> Or prey, or get—is it not lewd
> That we be eaten by our food
> And slept by sleepers in our sleep?

> (*SG*, 21; *NSP*, 61)

Through the reflexion and inversion of the primary
image, the dichotomy of thinking man is set forth: the self
viewed as subject and object, as predator and prey. This
pattern of reflexion and inversion can be abbreviated as
follows: "fleece"–"Fleece"–"golden sheep"–"prey, or get"–
"eaten" ("preyed upon")–"food" ("sheep")–"slept"–"sleep-
ers"–"sleep." By inverting the primary image, the poet
implies the inward direction the argosy will take. However,
he seeks the definition of his essence, not only in personal
and subjective terms, but also in terms of a kind of
Jungian "collective unconscious," mirrored in the vast
mythology of human experience.

Burke's analysis of the pattern of inversion illuminates
the poem sequence from another perspective, for he regards
the poems as a "dialectic of transcendence." Through the

19. Ibid., pp. 117–18.

pattern of inversion, "perception" becomes "reception," and "knowing," a "kind of sufferance," as if "the body were treading upon the mind."[20] Burke describes the poet's imaginative method as follows: "If the moods of the Self are translated into a corresponding imagery of sensation, then the duplication without can be experienced as imposing itself upon the sensibilities of the experiencer. Rhetorically: such doubling allows for the dignification of the Self; for if the poet (agent) is solemnly translated into terms of nature (scene), then in the reflexive sufferance of such scenes the poet's own mood would be like a spirit descending upon him, an annunciation. Here would be a dialectic of transcendence (a hierarchical wonder) whereby the poet could be infused by a transmogrification of himself."[21]

While Burke notes that the "purpose behind the imagery is psychological and intellectualistic, a venture in self-portraiture," one may add that this type of imagery is characteristic of Nemerov and is particularly effective in two ways: different images can be used to express the same mood or attitude, and, equally important, a single image can be bent to reflect multiple attitudes and feelings. The poem sequence is, indeed, a subjective venture, but the poet is never isolated from the poem's situation, although he may be divided within it.

The predatory-acquisitive theme, stated in Poem I, is repeated in III, IV, VI, and VIII, and is interwoven with subthemes. The "fall" motif (a favorite one with Nemerov), which also has inverse significance (fall = elevation), is set up in II, where the space-time continuum is designated as that of a dream—a journey to the center, or to the farthest circumference, which is the same thing.[22] The poet will seek to define his selfhood in both external and internal

20. Ibid., p. 117.
21. Ibid.
22. Ibid.

idioms: "Sleep in the zero, sleep in the spore / Beyond the
fires of Orion's hair." In "Beginning a falling dream" Burke
finds even a double intonality—a fall within a fall—suggested by the idea of falling asleep and dreaming of a fall.
Here, "fall" is associated with the stream of consciousness,
the "liquid brain," which encompasses the flux of time and
is "the flowing continuum of the individual's vital existence."[23] Implied here also is the "fall from grace" and its
inverse meaning, "elevation through another grace."[24] The
successive falls and ascensions, which move the poem from
one motivational realm to another, occur in V, VI, and VII,
which relate in various ways to the theme of absolute
guilt.[25] This theme is repeated in the ocean context of XI
and XII and in the final ascension of XVII, when the split
self becomes one with the world. Perhaps, the only "typical
moment" that Burke fails to note is the subtheme of free-
dom-imprisonment, or freedom-necessity, which is also an
underlying theme in "The Salt Garden." The reflexive inversion of the wild, secret beast (lion = city), whose stone
sinews tremble with strength (IV), occurs in IX, in which
"the caged sea / Knocks at the stone and falls away / . . .
Pacing to be free." The poet associates being shut in with
"the tunnel" (XI), as opposed to "free engines" (which
also "Race to burn themselves up"). Within the same poem,
the mind sheds its scales as the body is confined:

> In long halls of hospital, the white
> Eye peeled beneath the pool of light. . . .

But vision/blindness is temporary, for XII returns to the
water cave below the root—another fall and another elevation to come.

The ascension theme takes the form of a journey to the
deepest point within and to the farthest point without,

23. Ibid., p. 118.
24. Ibid.
25. Ibid., p. 120.

both of which are joined at the end of the poem. Moving from self (sleep) to city (stone, iron, earth underground), the poet escapes to (and is closed in by) the ocean world, the source of purgation and renewal. Ultimately, mind transcends body, through space and time, to the distant images of sun and moon, the symbols of the poet's two natures, which become as one. While sun may signify the male aspect and moon, the female aspect, predicated by the image of Tiresias (XVII), these figures may, also, signify time past and time future (Tiresias was a seer), with the moon being the dead past and the sun the living moment. Sun may also be identified with the substance of ocean (life), while the moon may be related to the city. As the moon is lit by the sun, so are the salt-vines underground fed, indirectly, from the ocean's substance. The merger of sun and moon, which is visually and symbolically an eclipse, must be conceived as a moving image. The idea of being-becoming is verified in XVIII, and in XVII the verbs, not the nouns, are accented.

> Then all was the self, but the self was none;
> Knowing itself in the fiery dark
> The blind pool of the eye became
> The sailing of the moon and sun
> Through brightness melted into sky.

The pattern of reflexion and inversion is reinforced by several technical devices which are observable elsewhere in Nemerov's work and which are analyzed by Burke in his explication. One device involves the use of a nexus of certain words which have visual, audial, and connotative similarities, as, for example, "skull"-"scales" (with the double meaning of "scales" implied), "eyes"-"I," "sleep"-"sheep," "veins"-"vines," "mined"-"mind," and the nexus of "caul," "gulls," "girls," and "galling," which echoes "skull" and "scales."

Another device is the use of a dominant color throughout the poem. In this case, white images are prevalent: the city, "white lion among waters," the "white grits" of Dutch Cleanser in the (also white) tub, "bleached virginity," "snow," "the white eye," "White shore and sky." This lack of contrast and blandness of scene enhances the inverted mood and the various conditions in the poem such as drowsiness, sleep, blindness, the sense of guilt and wish to be cleansed, the feeling of ennui, the willing of forgetfulness, or of ice, upon the self, and, at the end of the poem, the blinding whiteness of vision.

Perhaps the most ingenious device that Nemerov employs is what Burke terms "the narrative epigram." Burke indicates the subtle way in which Nemerov resorts constantly, but not obtrusively, to "incidental musicality (assonance, repetition, alliteration, and the like)" and adds that "such minor correspondences and variations of sound add eventfulness, in that they make for much bracketing of words, a bracketing also got by a gift for what we might call the 'narrative epigram'; 'the hushed flakes fell all day' would be an instance of both (the primal tonal welding would be in the fl, f—l augmentation of 'flakes fell')."[26]

As a poem sequence, "The Scales of the Eyes" is more promising than perfect. The manipulation of images is extremely complex and, in Burke's words, "the mythic use of nature-imagery sometimes becomes an obstruction, through the profusion of images, and through the profusion of overtones in one image."[27] The poem obviously cannot be grasped in a single reading and, because of its complexity, is better understood when read and pondered visually than when listened to. Yet the poems are the unique effort of a highly sensitive and thoughtful intelligence. As Burke concludes, when the poet's idiom is thought through, "it is found to have obeyed a subtle and scrupulous set of literary

26. Ibid., p. 128.
27. Ibid., p. 129.

laws that bring together, eloquently, many motivational strands basic to a poetic eschatology."[28]

Poem XVII, partially quoted above, summarizes almost all that is fundamental about Nemerov's use of interrelated elemental images. Throughout the sequence, desiccation has been associated with the confined space, the mined underground of the city with its stone sinews and iron nerves, and with the "crabbed house," the spiral shell, and the hospital. Rebirth occurs in the water context (water, snow, and ice) and pertains not only to the body—to feeling and sensation—but also to the mind as it transcends its bodily limitations in imagery of light and dark. Vision is, paradoxically, also blind—a state in which feeling becomes important—and the moment of convergence between mind and body, mind and physical world, is attained through imagination (a kind of natural grace)—"the blind pool of the eye" from which images spring. Thus, the poetry of space and light is that instant when form and substance become one in the flash across the gap of being above the dark abyss of eternity. That moment is:

Fire in the diamond,
Diamond in the dark.

("One Way," in *BS*, 86)

28. Ibid., p. 131.

4

THE THIRD VOICE

Nowhere is Nemerov's vision more beautifully conceived than in "Runes," which may be the greatest poem by an American poet in the twentieth century. Epic in scope, timeless in meaning, and representing a subjectivity "as nearly as possible universal in character," "Runes" could only have been written by a poet of our time. Metaphorically, the poem synthesizes all aspects and attitudes of the contemporary mind: religious, philosophical, scientific, and psychological. The poem is an odyssey of mankind and of the poet himself; its mood is alternately reflective and apathetic, tragic and comic, despairing and hopeful. Yet, like all great poems, "Runes" is a revelation of past, present, and future—"the story of the night told over."

The prophetic voice in the poem, "the third voice," is heard by poet and reader alike. "Runes" has had an appreciative audience of readers and critics, although they have dwelled more on the artistic and scientific merits of the poet's imagery than on the vision articulated. Vision, perhaps, is an archaic notion, but it is possible that reverence still exists. Even the most Philistine among us is wary of touching the ark, or refrains from dancing before it as David did. Among his own poems, "Runes" is Nemerov's

favorite,[1] yet he is reticent about it. He mentions it only
briefly in the very candid *Journal of the Fictive Life,* in the
passage on "eye, pond, and camera" cited earlier. When
the poem was praised to its author, he remarked that "it's
the kind of poem every poet wants to write," adding that it
was written during two successive weekends with little
revision.[2] The prophetic experience of "Runes," shared by
poet and reader, is miraculous enough not to require analysis. Significantly, Nemerov speaks of the poem as religious
—which it is in the broad sense of the word, being primarily concerned with the mystery of creation.

   Like "The Scales of the Eyes," "Runes" is a poem
sequence, based on exploration, which involves the relation
of mind and world attained through imagination. Each
poem sequence follows a "fall and ascension" theme of its
own, conveyed through elemental imagery, and each con-
cerns the loss of self (by the willing of snow upon the self
and a "going under") through which purgation, rebirth,
and revelation occur. In both sequences the doubling of
imagery correlates subjective with objective, or internal
with external. The pattern of reflexion and inversion
appears in both poems, as do the poet's unique natural idiom
and his use of the narrative epigram which combines words
that are visually, aurally, and connotatively alike.

   Yet "Runes" is a far greater poem than "The Scales of
the Eyes," chiefly because of their differences. "The Scales
of the Eyes" is the argosy of a younger poet, seeking identity, or selfhood, whose individual style is just beginning to
emerge. "Runes" is the odyssey of a more mature poet who
has found himself and, now, searches for meaning in the
world around him. Although both poems proceed on a circular space-time continuum, the earlier poem follows the
logic of a dream, or stream of consciousness, whereas

   1. Meinke, *Howard Nemerov,* p. 24.
   2. Nemerov responded thus when I praised the poem during one
of our conversations in January 1968.

"Runes" revolves on the relative theory of space-time and includes the linear dimension of recorded history. While the introspective theme of "The Scales of the Eyes" gives full rein to the poet's imagination, the imagery is so profuse, literary, subjective, and intricate that the reader cannot always share the poet's experience, particularly at a first reading. On the other hand, "Runes" evolves from three basic universal images which, even though they may be interpreted on several levels, are clearly and objectively configured throughout the poem. In spite of its literary references and general complexity, "Runes" is immediately experienced by the reader and, like all great poems, unfolds new meanings on each successive reading. The vast scope, depth, and universal significance of "Runes," combined with its organic beauty and clarity and simplicity of style, which the mature poet has achieved, make the poem Nemerov's finest literary achievement.

"Rune" literally means "a secret or mystery" and stems from two similar Old Norse and Old English words which probably derive from the Latin word "rumor." Runes are characters of the alphabet used in the oldest form of Germanic writing. They have been discovered as inscriptions on objects of wood, metal, and stone. The first authentic inscriptions were found in the boglands of Denmark and date back to the third century A.D. For years scholars have disputed the origin and history of the runic alphabet. Consensus is that runes were first used to give a fixed form to the spoken language. Later, they came to be used for magical purposes and associated with incantation.

As a title, "Runes" represents the secret and mysterious—the inscription of man's attempt to relate thought and thing. The title also suggests the possibilities and limitations of language as a mirror of nature.

The subtitle of the poem, "insaniebam salubriter et moriebar vitaliter" (St. Augustine, *Confessions*), literally translates as "in good health, I was seized by madness and, full of life, I was dying." A better translation, in terms of the original context, might be: "healthy in body, I was sick in soul; it was a living death."

The title and subtitle present, respectively, the universal and personal spectrum of the poem. Within the circular space-time continuum, which is universal and eternal, the temporal-linear dimension moves from past to present (B.C. to A.D.), covering the history of Western man. The theme, set forth in Poem I, is the mystery of Creation: "the stillness in moving things, / In running water, also in the sleep / Of winter seeds. . . ." In the mutability of generative substance and form, the poet seeks nature's inscriptions. This is man's timeless search for the secret of life and death in nature's hidden laws. Revelation happens when the mind, unable to penetrate the unknown, yields to the infinite mystery and becomes one with it. Regeneration, both spiritual and physical, occurs in the poem and is rendered in external, objective terms of the natural world which correspond to the subjective fluctuations of the poet's mood. The major achievement of "Runes," apart from the vision articulated, is the integration of external with internal, of body and mind, through which all paradox is resolved.

The wholeness of vision is accomplished by Nemerov's skillful treatment of three basic reflexive images which are multivalent, with such universal meanings that they may be interpreted on the scientific, philosophical, and psychological levels. The objective images, which pertain to body or matter, are water and seed—the generative substance and generative form of life, both of which are essential to creation. The subjective image, symbolic of mind, is "thought," the "trader doubly burdened, commercing / Out of one stillness and into another" (lines 14–15). Here, the reflexive pattern is stated. First, thought is "of something and the thought of thought" (line 13); therefore, thought seeks its object but is also the subject of itself. Secondly, thought is burdened by the stillness of past and future, yet does not exist in the present. Through reflexibility, man is aware of mutability, of paradox in all phenomena, and of the most perplexing paradox of all—thought, itself! Thought is the unifying image, moving between past and future, thought and thing, and all of the many other paradoxes of the human condition touched upon in the poem. As trader and explorer, thought pilots the ship of life across the sea of eternity. Limited by the laws of nature, thought may still travel the world in space and time, although it must return to itself, where it sees its reflection in nature (XIII) or in the mirror of the mind (XIV).

The form of "Runes" is organic, following the pattern of inversion and reflexion established by the imagery. A dynamic (or generative) and ritualistic effect is produced by the overall centripetal-centrifugal movement, which accentuates the circular space-time dimension. This effect is largely achieved by the inverse arrangement of the fifteen poems of the sequence in respect to content and imagery. Poem XV parallels I, figuratively, and resolves it; Poem XIV relates in the same way to II, XIII to III, and so on, with VIII standing alone at the core of the sequence. In VIII the poet reaches the depths of despair and sinks under; it is the moment of self-submission through which purgation occurs, followed by rebirth and revelation.

Other features contribute to the generative, ritualistic, and circular movement of the poem. The sequence turns on the annual cycle, moving from late summer to spring. Thought, associated with Ulysses (II), is middle-aged and identified with the surfeited time of year (August) through the images of traders and sunflowers in the third poem. Thought changes with the seasons, from summer to autumn (V), then to winter (VI, VIII) and the breaking of winter (X), followed by spring (XII, XV). Each of the poems consists of fifteen lines in iambic pentameter (the subtitle is incorporated in I), but each has its own tonal pattern. The poet's skillfull use of enjambment, occasional end rhyme, internal rhyme, assonance, and alliteration proceeds from image and mood as he goes from meditation to despair and apathy and finally to loss of consciousness, after which hope is revived.

The reflexivity of thought is maintained in the linear structure, as well as in the theme, of "Runes." In II the duality of thought is expanded into the images of Homer's and Dante's Ulysses, which represent two alternative ways of thinking and doing and establish the odyssey subtheme of the poem. Homer's Ulysses projects the acquisitive, materialistic, object-seeking aspect of mind, while Dante's Ulysses is mind searching to acquire virtue and knowledge. The acquisitive, appetitive theme, identified with corporeal motives, is developed in III, V, VII, IX, XI, and XIII. The spiritual, or philosophical, theme (where thought becomes the subject of itself) interacts with the acquisitive theme and is reflected in IV, VI, X, XII, and XIV. Thus, thought is conveyed moving reflexively through time, between mind and body, object and subject, until flesh and spirit are one and self becomes one with the world in XV.

The odyssey subtheme may be briefly summarized. Each journey, as an end in itself, is circular but leads to revelation. Man, the trader (III) and empire builder (XIII), is governed by the same laws of mutability as nature. Seeds mature to become sunflowers, which grow to such fullness that they fall under their own weight. Man, as trader, becomes the victim of his possessions; men seed commonwealths which grow into empires, overexpand, and fall apart (III, XIII). Material abundance is accompanied by spiritual emptiness; the fat time of the year is also the time of the atonement, yet man has nothing to offer but the "dry husk of an eaten heart" (V). Man's problem is his inability to accept nature's bounty and to be one with his source. God's presence is in everything, yet man has misused and misread the meaning of God in the natural process.

Knowledge derived from the Fall in Eden has taught man
"death" and the abuse of power, followed by guilt and
retribution. Man has perpetuated death, not life, through
the sacrifice of flesh and by making God into a human
image (XI). Having watered down form and substance in
our dehydrated time, man is unregenerative (VII); recognizing the danger of our explosive age, he is aware of the
need for faith and renewal (IX). Weighted down by his
own guilt and despair, man sinks (VIII) and becomes
identified with the lowest small creatures, the hunted convict, and the dead hunter (the hound). Through the cleans-
ing of the flesh by the dark, dirty water of death (which is
also the "soapy, frothing water"), man begins to hope (IX)
and to believe in God's immanence in all things (XI) and
recognizes his dual nature mirrored on the sea of eternity
(XIII). The mighty ocean is the great preserver and
destroyer of material form. All rivers lead to the sea, carrying with them the waste of continents. Man's seed is sewn
on land, fulfills its promise and decays; his dreams end in
the sea. Yet the mighty ocean, from all of the wreckage
poured into her, constantly renews the dry land and recon-
stitutes life in its myriad forms. On the surface of the ocean,
man sees his reflection and his shadow soul, Cain—the
destroyer who would also "seed a commonwealth in the
Land of Nod."

The search for virtue and knowledge leads to the limits
of mind's relation with the world—imagination. Through
thought, man is divided, and truth is paradoxical. One cannot apprehend reality. The secret of the seed, extracted by
knowledge, is death (IV), though it is also life (XII). All
logic and abstract thought is circular, ultimately leading to
the point of madness (VI). Yet through the loss of consciousness (or reflexivity), brought on by the willing of
snow upon the self, mind yields to oblivion and is renewed
by the dark, purifying water of death (VIII). With the
breaking of the ice, winter ends. The mind remembers

spring and imagines, in the fresh water tumbling downhill, the return of childhood innocence and joy (X). In the generative cycle and the symbiotic relationship of tree and bird, there is hope and the promise of life to come. Our human span is a stream, partaking of the raindrop and the sea— partaking of time and eternity (XII). Through imagination, the mind's eye creates the world in art—not reality but its image, temporal and fleeting as human life (XIV). Yet, through imagination, man sees, if only in a watered cloth with dissolving figures, the form and substance of what he is.

Our dual nature is mirrored on the sea of eternity. All that mind can know of reality comes to us through imagination and art. Truth, as perceived by man, is paradoxical. It cannot be known; it must be lived. Mind, moving between subject and object, past and future, can only be resolved in the present by ceasing to be reflexive. The secret of life and death is within us as in all of nature—a Bluebeard's room, which it is death to open, as man's history since Genesis reveals. Through total acceptance of the divine mystery in the act of being, spirit and flesh become whole and man is at one with nature, at one with his source.

RUNES, I

The theme is set forth in its several aspects: the mystery of Creation, of life, death, and mutability, and the paradox in all phenomena perceived by the mind in its reflexive relation with the world. Three basic images convey the theme and will be configured throughout the poem sequence: (1) water, the generative substance of life; (2) seed, the generative form; and (3) thought, ". . . A trader doubly burdened commercing / Out of one stillness and into another." Seed and water, the essential elements of procreation, will be used most often in combination, signifying regeneration (or the lack of it) in both a physical and metaphysical sense, for the poet's lens is double: he views with the scientific eye of the naturalist and with the mind's eye which probes the inscape of things. Thought, being objective and subjective ("The thought of something and the thought of thought"), is reflexive but ultimately defeated "before its object." Limited in space and time, thought cannot penetrate the mystery of being—the interval between past and present (lines 14–15). Through the simplest but most fundamental elements in nature, the poet projects his vast and complex theme: the universal, eternal mystery of ALL and NOW encircling the linear dimension, or diameter, where thought begins and ends in space and time and where perspective can only be paradoxical. Accordingly, thought will move between the two polar directions of the mind—outward to the silent void and inward to the dark interior of Self.

Organically, the theme develops with a centripetal-centrifugal force which springs from the tensions of paradox compressed in the three images: motion/stillness, time past/time future, form/substance, visible/invisible, sound/silence, being/nonbeing, and body/mind. Through the nexus of these multivalent images, meaning expands. For example, in lines 4–5 ("where time to come has tensed / Itself . . .") a double meaning evolves. On the spatial level, the future form is compacted ("tensed") inside the present form of the seed. On the temporal level, the future tense is implicit in the present—i.e., becoming is part of being. In lines 5–6, the "hourglass" has the dual aspect of a microscope and the passage of time, suggesting that nature's secret inscription is written microscopically inside the seed, now, but that time alone can magnify the prospective form and essence of that secret. Again, in lines 6–7, double meanings derive from "unfold" and "sentence." "Unfold" refers to the uncoiling of the radix from the seed, as its cover breaks and germination occurs, and to the revelation of what is locked in its chromosomal material. "Sentence" can be construed as the destiny inherent in the seed (its genetic code) and also as its linear inscription in time (its life span). Finally, the last eight lines establish the various ways of the mind which will recur in the sequence: (1) the reflexivity of thought (as in the mirror image); (2) thought as a sailor (an adventurer or wanderer) of uncharted seas who always returns to port; and (3) thought, with its appetitive and acquisitive leanings, trading on past and future possibilities. The poem begins and ends in mystery and silence.

The contrapuntal tonal pattern used in the first poem undergoes variation in later poems. The first seven lines, strongly musical and onomatopoetic, form the leitmotif of subsequent lines which focus on the mystery of nature. In contrast to the leitmotif, the last eight lines are almost prosaic except for the feeling of weight produced through repetition and through the trader image (lines 14–15). The discursive tone here will recur later whenever thought is subjective and separated from the natural world.[3]

RUNES, II

The odyssey theme begins with the image of Ulysses, an extension of the dual image of thought in the first poem. Two ways of thinking and being are illustrated through the two Ulysses (Homer's and Dante's). Homer's Ulysses (lines 1–9), the man of action, compromises with life or, in current vernacular, "plays the game." After his adventurous years at war and at sea, he settles down to the "normal" life of a country squire—a life of ease and luxury not always honestly achieved (lines 7–8). On the other hand,

---

3. Here, as elsewhere, enjambment, present participles, and soft vowels are used to achieve fluidity. Stillness is effected through alliteration of the double *e* combined with *s* (e.g., "sleep of winter seeds"). Tension is caught in lines 5–6 through repetition of clipped consonants (*t*, *m*, *n*, and *d*), especially *t*, and through quick, short phrases. The extension of time is accentuated by the long *o* and by the unbroken iambic beat in the following lines: "only / The years unfold its sentence from the root." As in the rest of the sequence, richness of sound is created through internal rhyme ("sleep"-"seed," "time"-"fine") and assonance ("root"-"but," "defeat"-"thought").

Dante's Ulysses follows the lonely, courageous, and independent course of thinking man—the pursuit of knowledge and virtue. Pushing thought beyond the bounds of common sense and practicality to the point of madness, ". . . Drowning near blessed shores he flames in hell. . . ." The gates (or pillars) of Hercules (line 11) were the known western limits of the ancient world and, in this context, signify the limits of human knowledge. In following the westward course of the sun (symbolic of the light of the mind), Dante's hero goes beyond mortal limits and falls, as it were, off the face of the earth. Two alternative ways of the mind are available, both of which are hazardous. The dilemma is underscored in the last line: "I do not know which ending is the right one." The gods seem to favor those who help themselves, yet man becomes Promethean in his efforts (and through his fall) in the pursuit of knowledge. The tone of this poem, befitting its theme, is that of a philosophical dialogue—discursive and matter-of-fact.

RUNES, III

The way of Homer's Ulysses is expanded in this poem, which, unlike II, is rich in tone and texture,[4] for the subject is man's lust for material objects. Here, thought is a trader (representing the acquisitive motives of mind) and is identified with the sunflower—an extension of the seed—which embodies the sensual, surfeited aspects of greed at-

---

4. Musically, the indolent quality at the beginning of the poem is produced by a lack of enjambment which allows the singsong iambic pentameter to have a lulling effect, deepened by the assonance of end rhyme ("time"-"gain") and by internal rhyme ("deep"-"sleepy"). Other nuances are created through internal rhyme: "shore"-"more" (lines 6–7), and "sun"-"down"-"ground" (lines 7–8). The repeated *r* accentuates the onomatopoeia of lines 5–6: "bare," "raking," "true," "crack," "driving," "your," "wreckage," "world," "shore." The meaning of the last six lines is enhanced by sibilance. All but one of the five forceful verbs begin with *s*: "strangled," "stripped," "spill," and "spend." A crescendo of the *s* sound begins in line 10 and culminates in the alliteration of lines 14–15 ("savage . . . spill," and "spend . . . silver").

tached to objects. Both mind and body (subject and object, trader and sunflower) pursue the sun not as the light of reason but as the source of earth's produce. The theme is carried through multivalent imagery, almost all of which is yellow or golden, heavy, round, hard, and dry—suggesting weight, waste, and decay. Man, like the sunflower, falls under the weight of his material burden and is stripped of his gain. Only then does he learn "how charity / Is strangled out of selfishness at last. . . ."

The interplay of images is exceedingly complex here. In the first two lines the double image indicates the mood, the situation, and the time of day and year, in terms of indolence, excess, and slow decay. The "rounding" of "the horn of time" conveys multiple meanings through the figure of "the horn" in connection with "time." (Significantly, one definition of horn is "the end of a cresent." A horn or cresent is alluded to, either literally or figuratively, in II, III, V, and XIV.) The "rounding of the Horn" (Cape Horn, the southernmost point of South America) has always been dreaded by sailors because the region is so stormy. The Horn of Plenty, when too full (rounded), spills its contents. The biblical horn symbolizes strength, honor, and glory, which, when excessive, lead to pride—and to a fall. The point in time, too, is ominous: the lull before the storm and the sleepy hour of the day in late summer when vegetation is most lush—before it begins to die. How skillfully the poet paints, with a single stroke, the wreckage of sunflowers and traders (lines 3–6)—the west wind that will fell the flowers in autumn and strew the ships' remains "on the world's lee shore." (The sense of waste is heightened further by the irony of line 6.) The description of "bare pole's cracking works equally well for the headless stems physical meanings converge again in lines 7–10, for "truth" and for the stripped masts of the ships. Physical and meta- is heavy and the act of bowing beneath it suggest humility, as well as physical and moral collapse. The "golden miser" metaphor (lines 11–15) has many nuances. The "courts of summer" imply the artificial life of the trader, which is qualified more fully in the remaining lines. Line 12 suggests that one cannot make the world one's object and that amassing money ("coining images") is fruitless because money, per se, is a worthless image on a coin. Lines 13–15 recapitulate the poem's imagery. The "quarter of the wheel" connotes the season of the year, money on the wheel of fortune, the quarter of the ship's wheel, and the circular dry mass of the fallen sunflower head. "Broken," obviously, has triple meaning in connection with the wheel and refers to a spiritual and physical (material) condition. "Savage ground" is not merely the jungle of the world but is also the uncultivated land where the seeds of wealth and the sunflowers' pollen are strewn by the winds of chance. The last two lines reiterate the metaphor of wasted seed; "tarnished silver" signifies bad seed and bad money. This final image derives from Genesis 38:9: "And Onan knew that the seed should not be his; and it came to pass, that when he went unto his brother's wife, that he spilled it on the ground, lest that he should give seed to his brother."

RUNES, IV

The way of Dante's Ulysses is expanded here, where philosophical thought (the search for virtue and knowledge) ends with the knowledge of death. Nature's message is death, inscribed on seed and stone. Death is the human condition, physically and spiritually, as revealed in Genesis and in the seed of the forbidden fruit of the Tree of Knowledge. Death is the starting point; "the family tree / Grows upside down . . ." as tombstone inscriptions verify. In this poem the seed is configured always in terms of death: the cock's egg (egg of the serpent and egg of being), the stone (pit and tomb), and the Tree of Knowledge. Water, as generative substance, is missing; seed is associated with fire (line 1) and blood (line 15). Thought has fatal consequences, as did the egg hatched by the serpent and the plot hatched by Satan.

The deft use of simple objects having multiple significance (e.g., "pit," "stone," "tree"), and the close interweaving of biblical and mythical imagery, make this an intricate but intriguing poem. The context of seed (life) is death. In line 1, "The furnaces of death" connote the womb and hellfire. Death is inherent in the seed, first, and then in the egg. The "cock's egg" has several interrelated meanings. To many ancient peoples the egg symbolized creation, reality, or being. More specifically, the egg can be associated with the basilisk, the legendary serpent who was hatched from the egg of a seven-year-old cock. The basilisk is said to have a cock's head, an animal's body, and a serpent's tail; his glance and breath are fatal. Thus, this figure can be extended to incorporate that of Satan in the Garden. The hatching of the basilisk parallels the plot hatched by Satan when he had taken the form of a snake. The serpentine figure winds through word and image in the first eight lines, carrying a complex of meanings. Lines 3–5 place all time in the present tense—NOW—but NOW is death, not life. "Wintry coil" and "spring so tight" (line 3) describe not only the serpent (who is synonymous with death), but also the perennial condition of man. "Wintry" implies the buried past (what is dead), while "spring" suggests what is coiled and about to be released—the deadly future. Lines 3–5 present an inversion of the seed image in I, lines 3–6. The mystery of the seed is now dispelled. The hourglass (I, line 5) will not magnify the genetic code within the seed, nor will the years unfold it. What exists in the seed, as in the serpent, is explicit—the eternal presence of death. Here, one must accept the adjective "radical" in its most basic sense, for, in this context, it refers to the radix of the seed—that part which erupts first through the seed cover and germinates. The "radical presence" is such "that every tense / Is now." The metaphor in lines 5–9

compounds the preceding image as the theme moves from
the circular to the linear dimension—man's recorded history. (This transition in thought is denoted quite literally
by the uncoiling of the serpent as his evil plot unwinds.)
Knowledge (reason, language, order) perpetuates the seeds
of truth sown in Eden; Satan's design and its consequences
are eternalized through his seed. "Sentences" in line 7 takes
on the double inference of I, line 6, but with implications of
guilt and atonement, for the voice here is that of subjective
man thinking. The "scripture's pith" (line 8) can be interpreted as the core of the forbidden tree and as the meaning of the Word (the breath). "In rooted tongues" refers
to the serpent and his seed and to the death of innocence
in Eden from which knowledge (guilt) preserved through
language, derived. Line 9 reiterates the thought of line 1
that our fate is sealed by death even before life begins. In
the last six lines, the tree (which "grows upside down")
has several aspects. It is the forbidden tree, of course, but
also a scriptural tree; the genealogy, extending from Adam
to Christ, begins and ends with death or, put another way,
commemorates death, not life. "The family tree" has other
meanings which are both general and specific. Universally,
it represents human history, where lie the "buried stones"
philosophers have sought and never found—the stones
whose secret is death without regeneration, for they issue
blood, not water (line 15). In a more literal sense, the
family tree grows "upside down," whether inscribed on
paper or on the stone marker of the family plot; the list of
names reads from top to bottom chronologically. Perhaps,
"iconically," this bears out the biblical truth (Matthew 20:
16) that "the last will be first, and the first last." The message of the poem is powerfully condensed in the final narrative epigram. All faith in life is nullified through the
mordant inversion of the most basic Hebrew and Christian
concepts; the dark vision of death extends even beyond
doubt.[5]

5. Tension is built up in the first five lines through sibilance

Runes, V

The theme of death is followed by that of guilt and atonement without regeneration. The odyssey of Homer's Ulysses continues into autumn—the "fat time of the year," which is also "the time of the Atonement." Natural plenty is contrasted with spiritual emptiness. No rebirth occurs as the poet sinks deeper into despair and apathy over the futility of life. Lush, bountiful images of nature (lines 1–6) are paralleled by hard, dry, desolate images of the human condition (lines 7–15). In the first three lines the seed is manifested in the full berry bushes where birds flock. Here is the happy simplicity of the natural generative cycle—the symbiotic relationship between bird and bush. On the other hand, man cannot enjoy nature's blessings without abusing them or without guilt and atonement. For him the undecipherable seed is hid in the nothingness (the "zero") of life, which is all that the "dry husk of an eaten heart" can offer up in atonement.

Again, the poet uses multivalent imagery, some of which is biblical, to convey the idea of natural plenty and spiritual emptiness. The contrast between man's material and spiritual condition is explicit in the first six lines. "Judgment" or "sentence" (which is connected to the seed as in I and IV) weighs heavy in lines 3–4. Man must "answer for" his harvest and its depletion; he must atone for what he has reaped (and sown) and what he cannot sow (or reap) in the wintry future. The next two lines abound in sensuous imagery. The "slain legal deer" has a touch of

---

and the alliteration of *s* and through quick, sharp phrases and clipped consonants (*c*, *t*, *p*, *d*). Coldness and evil are conveyed by sound and alliteration in the phrase "Wound in his wintry coil." Assonance is effective in producing a sense of conflict and in stressing the relationship between words and between pairs of words, as follows: "serpent"-"tense," "fruit"-"sought," "word"-"seed"-"blood." The repetition of key words in the last four lines ("stone," "word," "flesh," "seed") accentuates the cyclical nature of death. Lines 13–14 form what Kenneth Burke calls a "narrative epigram": "each word / Will be made flesh, and all flesh fall to seed. . . ." The tonal pattern here is built on *fl* and *f—l* and on internal rhyme for emphasis ("all"-"fall").

irony, intimating that atonement might be made for many
deer slain out of season. Also implied is man's relationship
with nature, which is not symbiotic but predatory and subject to man's, not nature's, laws. Lines 7–8 pertain to regeneration; their significance is primarily religious and
ritualistic, but with sexual overtones. The "ram's horn"
refers to the shofar which is sounded on Rosh Hashanah
but also symbolizes male sexual power. Both Rosh Hashanah
and Yom Kippur are implied in the poem. Rosh Hashanah
(which falls on the first day of the month of Tishri) is the
first day of the New Year and the first of the ten days of
penitence which end with Yom Kippur, the Day of Atonement and the holiest day in the Jewish calendar. "Obser-
vance" (line 9) extends the dual meaning of the "ram's
horn," but in a way which perhaps is peculiar to Nemerov,
who associates "seeing" with the sexual act and with guilt
(*Journal of the Fictive Life,* 81–85, 146–47). Both interpretations merge in their ritualistic, regenerative sense.
Emptiness, dryness, and meaninglessness are strong in the
last six lines. What remains from the past year's painful
abscess is all that the heart can offer—the cancelled-out
desires which were either unrealized or ended in disillusion-
ment. God's face, in "His winter's mercy," is hid; no
light exists in the winter of the soul. No promise of life to
come lies in the undecipherable seed—the "zero" which is
"naught." The poem ends with a succession of hollow figures: "dry husk," "eaten heart," "Abscess," "zero," and
barren "seed."[6]

6. Rhythmical and musical devices add a biblical resonance to
the poem and create a contrast between the lushness of nature and
man's spiritual emptiness. Meaning is enhanced in the first two
lines by the syntax, the repetition of "time," and the contrasting
effects of the alliterated *t*. In line 1, emphasis falls on "fat," which,
when sounded with "time," conveys the round, ripe richness of
autumn. The repeated *t* is necessarily enunciated briefly but vigor-
ously, whereas, in the phrase "time / Of the Atonement," the beat
falls on "time" and "-tone-," which, in conjunction with the repeated
m, the *n*, and long *o*, produce a solemn effect like the tolling of a bell.
The parallel phrasing of "time" echoes the parallel construction of

RUNES, VI

Here, subjective thought approaches the nihilistic state of blindness (the white agony of "The Scales of the Eyes"), expressed in images of white water and snow. The reflexivity between subject and object can go no farther outward or inward but is paralyzed. Thought sees "White water now in the snowflake's prison" and is, itself, imprisoned in the dead-end circularity of its own abstractions. The white chaos of order (the snowflakes falling) cannot be caught by the mind, nor can mind imprint for an instant its vision on the snow. Here the seed is abstracted first to the snowflake, then to the infinitesimal atom—the most fundamental of all forms, and the basis of substance as well. This particle marks the end of thought, "the defeat / Of thought before its object, where it turns / As from a mirror. . . ."

Almost all of the imagery in VI is hexagonal or circular, and abstract in the sense that it is either formal or unsubstantial. In progression, there are "the snowflake's prison," hexagonal thoughts (lines 2–3), "atoms of memory," "this distracted globe," "snowflakes" (again), "seeds," and, in synthesis, "the atom." Whiteness is everywhere in this poem. Paradox is here, too, but in terms of form itself; no two forms of anything are exactly alike (lines 3–4 and 7–9). Substance becomes form and form, substance (lines 10–12). Nature's abstractions (white water "in the snowflake's prison") mirror the hexagonal thoughts, the abstractions of the "mad king in a skull cap" trying to find meaning in chaos through endless introspection. The "riches of order snowed without end" are the reality that man cannot grasp in any way; he cannot "number" the flakes or

---

many of the psalms. Lines 7–8 are onomatopoetic and achieve solemnity through a succession of one-syllable words, suggestive of the notes of a horn. "Sounded," because it has two syllables, stands out forcefully. The alliterated h ("horn," "high") in these lines increases the sense of distance—the far heights from which the sound comes. Dryness is felt in the last six lines through sibilance (s, c, and z) and through the strong alliteration of r.

"fingerprint" them as they fall. "The atoms of memory" in Democritus' time had hooks at either end, connecting past to future in the Euclidian world of cause and effect. But, in the Einsteinian universe, reality is total, dynamic, and circular; all is contemporaneous, simultaneous, and beyond our vision. The correlated images of seed, snowflake, and atom merge in the last four lines. Form is indissolubly frozen in substance, forming a white mirror of the mind. Spring may be the form melting into substance beneath that snow, but this is a question. As in "The Scales of the Eyes," the poet wills snow and ice upon himself, seeking oblivion and blindness, through which purgation occurs and vision is restored.[7]

Runes, VII

The tone of this poem is witty and satirical, though the poet's mood is no less dark. The theme shifts from the desired oblivion at the end of VI ("White water, fall and fall") to our "dehydrated age"—the winter wasteland where the "zero" (of V, lines 14–15) has become transparent. The man of action, the corporeal man, is now "unstable as water" and impure because he has defiled both his seed and substance. Impotent and lacking in pride and strength, he can no longer create anything of value, either in life or in art. His synthetic world is artificial, watered down, and ineffectual. Here, again, is "the defeat / Of thought before its object, where it turns / As from a mirror," but this

7. Continuity and reflexivity of thought are sustained through enjambment and the succession of hexagonal parallel images. The tone is discursive but also desperate and questioning. The poem begins as a monologue and moves inward, ending with a question without answer. Here is the beginning of oblivion (the wish for it), which is peace. Soft vowels and consonants are used effectively in lines 9–12 to simulate the lightness of snow falling; one feels the flurries in the alliterated *f* and *fl*: "fingerprint," "flakes," "flight" (lines 9–10). Silence comes with the repeated *m*, *n*, and *s*: ". . . Moments melting in flight, seeds mirroring / Substance without position or a speed / And course unsubstanced."

time, thought is defeated before manmade objects which
reflect man's mind and the sterile world he has artifacted
out of the seed and substance of nature.

Because of its humor, clever punning, and contempo-
raneity, the poem is deceivingly simple at first glance, a
cutting commentary on modern life. (Perhaps this is why
it has been removed from context and anthologized.) However, the complex configurations of seed and water grow
out of the earlier poems of the sequence and are embedded
in the meaning of the opening quotation, Jacob's dying
blessing to Reuben, which should be read in the original
context to be fully understood.

> Reuben, thou art my firstborn, and my might, and the
> beginning of my strength, the excellence of dignity,
> and the excellence of power:
>
> Unstable as water, thou shalt not excel; because thou
> wentest up to thy father's bed; then thou defiledst it:
> he went up to my couch.

"Reuben, thou art my firstborn, and my might . . ."; that
is, the first fruits (also the sacrifice) and the seed that will
carry my power to the ends of the earth. You are born of
me and created in my image. But you have defiled thy
father's couch—mother earth—the place where you were
conceived. The voice in these lines is not simply that of an
irate father; it is the voice of a patriarch, the voice of Israel
through whom God speaks—a thundering voice whose re-
percussions shake the synthetic posture of civilization,
where "the last word and / The least word" have become
as nothing and "even the Muse / In her transparent raincoat, resembles a condom."

The seed ("zero") has been configured one step further
as the negative of zero—the transparent form of our empty
lives. Water, being mixed (therefore, impure) is no longer
a generative substance. Seed and water combine to produce

only synthetic effects, in every instance—whether in life or in art. Lacking substance, man is dehydrated, ". . . Nervously watering whisky and stocks, / Quick-freezing dreams into realities." "Stocks" can be read as a pun, as can "Quick-freezing dreams," with its various associations which go beyond the deep-freeze. The commercialism and artificiality decried here are ubiquitous enough not to need comment. Lines 7–12 allude to Proust's "Overture" (the first chapter of *Swann's Way*[8]), where the past returns to Marcel through the taste and smell of "the crumb of madeleine soaked in her decoction of lime flowers which my aunt used to give to me. . . ." In the same passage Proust recalls the Japanese paper flowers, crumbs "without character or form" which, when placed in water, stretch, bend, and take on color and shape. His recollections of the house at Combray are most appropriate as the bases of the metaphors here. No writer in the past hundred years (with the possible exception of Joyce) has been more sentient in expression than Proust. But, more importantly, he could experience the bittersweet sense of the past and recreate it, which contemporary man cannot do. Proust's memories contain the fragrance and taste of lime flowers, the touch, the shape, and the color of the Japanese flowers as they unfolded in water. Our madeleines are tasteless and odorless, for our senses have lost their power; without them we cannot evoke the past - or recreate the present. Only the "brain surgeons" can produce the "proustian syndrome"—by means of anesthesia or through psychoanalysis, perhaps. Unfeeling, we are detached in space and time. "The plastic and cosmetic arts / Unbreakably record" everything; no value exists in the medium (since it is "unbreakable") or in its subject (lines 12–13). The "word" and the "Muse" are traduced to nothing. She, dry in her plastic raincoat, is a commodity to be manufactured, bought (or sold), used, and thrown away; she is totally uncreative.[9]

8. Page 36.
9. Lack of musicality in the poem serves to intensify its mood,

RUNES, VIII

The darkest of the poems, VIII, is the turning point of the sequence—the loss of consciousness, or "the going under," and the death of self through which purgation and rebirth occur. The seed, as generative form, lies dormant in "the buried hulls of things / To come" and in "the sleeping roots" and "the breathing dreams / Of all small creatures sleeping in the earth. . . ." But these are future forms which will unfold. Here the seed ("zero's eye") is blacked out and merged with the "pit"—the pit of death where form and identity cease to be. Slithering through the poem, the stream, like the Greek hydra, is the dominant dark image, although it retains its positive significance.[10] The "water of dirt, water of death, dark water" is also the "soapy, frothing water" which carries away winter's debris and cleanses. With the fall into the stream of darkness, the stream of consciousness is lost, merging with the life sleeping underground. Rising again, only to sink deeper in the mire, man goes "on to the end / With the convict hunted through the swamp all night." Then, hunter and hunted become one— "the dog's corpse in the ditch," the lowest of all creatures. Yet in spite of the dark, stagnant images at the end of the poem ("swamp," "ditch," and "pit"), the hope of regeneration prevails in "the one / Still ebbing stream" and in the future forms sleeping in the earth. Winter is breaking now; ice melts into the stream which is replenished as it carries off the dirt-streaked floes. The naturalistic description of the changing stream augments the metaphysical sense of

tone, and meaning, all of which are dry and cynical. The satiric thrust in each figure or metaphor is emphasized through irony, puns, and antitheses. Pivotal words are accented through syntax, as, for example, "*Quick*-freezing," "dunk," "Muse." A sense of nervousness is maintained by irregularity in the meter. Polysyllabic and monosyllabic lines may alternate (e.g., lines 2–3, 7–8), and certain lines can take four beats as well as five (e.g., lines 4, 5, and 6), depending on where the stress is placed in the first foot.

10. If one visualizes the stream as Hydra, the Greek mythological serpent, then it would have the power of regenerating evil. My interpretation is less extreme, resting on the more general meaning of the hydra—i.e., "water serpent."

the poem; nature's season and the season of the heart are one. Like Thoreau, the poet feels the latent power and beauty of this season which is seldom eulogized in poetry or prose; he hears the stir of life underground beneath the cracking of the ice. He sees the future greenness in the "tangle of sleeping roots" and smells the fragrance of the "green Pinewoods." Through the dark water regeneration will come.

Water, as the sustaining image, is full of paradoxical meanings. Its dual function (generative/destructive) is established in two double images in lines 2–5. First, water is dark, "threading through / The fields of ice. . . ." Next, water is "soapy" and "frothing," slithering "under the culvert below the road, / Water of dirt, water of death, dark water. . . ." Water, as the vital force, seeps through the the roots of tree and bush and deep into the earth where creatures hibernate. But, in the last lines, water becomes the stagnant swamp and, ultimately, the ditch and the dank pit of death. As primordial substance, water is deeper than man's twin concepts of good and evil. In the present context, the serpentine aspect of the stream must dominate, because regeneration is just beginning in man and in nature. The vast dimensions of human experience reflected in Conrad's ocean (XIV) are now only dimly perceived; here is the immersion, not the reflection, of thought. Through this immersion, feeling is restored so that, in a Dostoevskian sense, man knows that he is alive *only* because he "*feels*"—however cold, damp, and humiliating that feeling is—after the numbness of winter (VII). Existing still on the linear plane of time (in the throes of the serpent death), man falls under his dual burden (as hunter and the hunted) but not to die, though "zero's eye is closed," for he will rise again with the prescience that life will come—out of the pit (seed) and the dark water.[11]

11. The movement of the poem, paralleling that of the stream, begins slowly, gains some momentum, then diminishes (lines 1–10)

RUNES, IX

The dry cynical tone of VII continues but diminishes in IX, for a feeling of potential energy (however negative) has returned after the purgative experience of VIII. The shift toward feeling is accomplished through nuances which subtly invert the meaning of the imagery in VII. The times are still "dehydrated," but, whereas before all was watered down and ineffectual, now everything is condensed yet retains some degree of power. As VII opened, the Old Testament figures provided the allegory of broken faith and loss of power through the defilement of seed and substance. Conversely, IX includes two allusions to parables in the Gospel and ends with the Christian figures Mary and St. Christopher, who signify the "humble power" that can carry the burden of living faith "in the world's floodwaters" (lines 13–15). Man's perversion of creative energy (lines 1–4) and of faith (lines 5–13) parallels the perversion of body and mind (seed and substance) in VII. But, in IX the possibility of physical and spiritual renewal is inferred through the respective figures of Mary and St. Christopher—a possibility that does not exist in VII.

before the fall (line 11). A brief rise and fall occurs in lines 12–13 —the last gasp, perhaps, before sinking. The final line falls heavy like a chord. Weight, weariness, sleep, and death are conveyed through sound as well as through the slow ebb and flow of the rhythm, which is restrained by means of a succession of infinitives: "To go low, to be as nothing, to die, / To sleep. . . ." (lines 1–2); "To come" (line 9), "To fall" (line 11), "to go on" (line 12) and "to come at last" (line 14). The repeated long *o* (lines 1–4) creates a sense of weight as does the repetition of a word ("water," line 5) or sound ("all"-"small"-"fall," lines 10–11). Visually and aurally, the narrative epigram (line 5) suggests darkness and heaviness: "Water of dirt, water of death, dark water," built on the tonal pattern w—d, w—d, and d—w. Where water is the life force (lines 6–10), movement accelerates and the sounds are softer. Line 9 is onomatopoetic, with softness in the alliteration of *s* in conjunction with the repeated *l*. In contrast is the next line with its heavy beat and monosyllabic stresses: "To fall with the weight of things down on the one." The poet's skillful transformation of mood and image in this poem is accomplished largely through his subtle ear and metrical control.

Unlike the bland imagery of VII, seed and water gain strength here, despite their synthetic or destructive connotations. Condensation, as an aspect of the present, is brought out through a succession of tightly compressed configurations of the seed: "pills," "atoms," "grain of wheat," "plastic tears," "mustard seeds," and "lucite lockets." All of these figures are hard, containing, in various degrees, the potential to expand or explode; all are unregenerative and/or destructive, since they are dehydrated. Water, too, is perceived as potentially destructive (line 14), although its generative power is implied in the final image. (I.e., one survives by moving with the flood, or being borne by it, not by swimming against it.) All allusions are inverted and are concisely ironic with a strong satirical barb. For example, lines 2–4 (referring to the current aphorism "dynamite comes in small packages") are a sharp comment on the perversity of thought, feeling, and expression, as well as on the materialism and the perversion of energy, in our age. Similarly, in lines 4–9, The Parable of the Sower (Matthew 13:3–8) and The Parable of a Grain of Mustard Seed (Matthew 13:31) are inverted to achieve a satiric effect. Likewise, the celluloid statues of Mary and St. Christopher are ironical: planted on car dashboards for "safety's sake," they are not only synthetic reproductions which appeal to our perverse minds, but are also a driving hazard.

As in VII, the lack of musicality reinforces mood, meaning, and tone, while satire is produced through irony, litotes, antitheses, and tragicomic paradox. In lines 1–12, understatement is highly effective as the poet moves from advertising to atoms with the cool detachment of a radio or television announcer. In contrast, the last three lines are forceful in their unequivocal simplicity; the recollection of the historical figures is significant, for mind is now relating to the past and in a positive way, which was not possible in VII.

RUNES, X

'e mystery of being remains a riddle to the mind but, now,
tion can be experienced through memory as feeling is
ed. The white waterfall (wished for in VI, line 15)
from its prison of ice to "render up the new / Chil-
ater. . . ." Form and substance, indissolubly frozen
: and, as the ice breaks, cascade forth in a daz-
zl. of remembered images. The poem becomes a
son, ng creation and the beginning of spring, hope,
and v, as inscribed on seed, stone, and tree (so
strong, f the earlier poems), is no more than a
shadow "A distant chill, when all is brought to
pass / By irth and rising of the dead."

Clues t ning of this poem lie in its sensuous
imagery (wh ments the cold imagery of VI) and
in the switch c line 5. In lines 1–5, white water
is in a transient 'ther wholly solid nor liquid but
the "feather of a 1 ween the stones." The question
remains: "is the rac tay / Or pass away?" Though
the water's "utteranc d," it is perceived as "rainbowed," "clear and col of stone." Blinded by the
water's brilliance but w nses awakened, the poet
recaptures vision through a waterfall of images,
all of which are regenerative w Children of water"
emerge "and their tumbling l hter runs down the
hills, and the small fist / Of the enches in the day's
dazzle. . . ."

The poet's unique gifts in cre ical and rhythmical effects are nowhere better e than in this
poem which bears out what Peter Mei of the entire
sequence: "The run-on blank verse line, ntly match
rhythm and content: a liquid sense tremb merov's]
lines." The tonal effects are strong here, ral imagery is dominant; every line is onomatopo

12. Lightness is effected in lines 1–3 through t ion of

RUNES, XI

While V conveys the fullness of nature and the spiritual
emptiness of man in the absence of God, XI shows awareness of God and the presence of the Creator in all things.
Different biblical images are used here to express the poet's
new mood. He is now sensitive to God's dynamic immanence in nature:

> A holy man said to me, "Split the stick
> And there is Jesus." When I split the stick
> To the dark marrow and the splintery grain
> I saw nothing that was not wood, nothing
> That was not God. . . .

The parallel phrases, "nothing that was not wood, nothing /
That was not God," with the apposition of "wood" and
"God" at the end of each phrase, make it impossible not to
mentally add the nexus "good," in reference to both "wood"
and "God." This association is indicated, yet the poet must
refrain from using "good" with its moral intonations, for
he is picturing God as beyond good and evil, as both a tran-
scendent and immanent power. That man has traditionally
conceived of God as a moral force (which is to say that he
has made God in his own image) is strongly implied in the
rest of the poem. What man learned through eating of the
Tree of Knowledge of good and evil brought death—a death
which we have perpetuated (through knowledge) in our-

---

wh, *w*, and *t*, and by the alliteration of *f*, *s*, and *r*. Brightness and
coldness are achieved through the reiterated *r* and long *o* in lines
3–5 ("riddled," "utterance," "rainbowed," "clear," "brilliance,"
"cold," and "stone"). The bubbling joyous quality of the water (and
children) is produced by the repetitive *t* and *l* and in the cascading
syllables of lines 5–11. In lines 9–10 ("the small fist / Of the seed
unclenches in the day's dazzle . . ."), the rhythm of the lines simu-
lates the action described. In the last two lines, the pale nebulous
imagery of cloud and shadow contrasts with the bright images of
preceding lines yet has a calmness that makes the earlier grey mood
of the sequence seem far behind.

selves and in the death of God on the Cross. The poet tells
us that God is *not* hidden; He exists in us and through us
as we are part of the total nature of the universe, not because of our acceptance or rejection of Him. The poet implies that God did not make evil or death, but that man did;
therefore, guilt is not atoned for by death. Death is part
of the natural process in which and through which God
is always present as the Supreme Reality.

The meaning of XI (which is further expanded in XII)
is borne out in the configurations of seed and water and in
the historical pattern which man's reflexivity (acquired in
Eden) has followed, as revealed in the Scriptures. The seed
(which produced the rod of the opening lines) becomes the
Tree of Knowledge (line 6); then, "Aaron's rod that
crawled in front of Pharoah"; and, later, Jesse's rod (lines
7–8), "flowering / In all the generations of the kings."
These Old Testament images all convey man's perversion
of knowledge and power. Next, the seed is transfigured into
the New Testament "second tree," the cross of Christ, and,
lastly, becomes "Adam's tainted seed":

> And came the timbers of the second tree,
> The sticks and yardarms of the holy three-
> masted vessel whereon the Son of Man
> Hung between thieves, and came the crown of thorns,
> The lance and ladder, when was shed the blood
> Streamed in the grain of Adam's tainted seed.

From this second tree, the symbol of the Atonement,
came also the "crown of thorns," "the lance," and "the lad-
der," which images again suggest man's perversion of natural objects so that God exists in the name of death, not
life. The fact that Christ is called "The Son of Man" instead
of by his more frequent title, "Son of God," emphasizes the
poet's implication that man has deified himself, or capital-
ized himself. The generative image of water becomes blood

at the end of the poem, connoting death with killing and sacrifice, the latter being a human tradition but not part of the natural process.

RUNES, XII

While IV carries the fatalistic message that death is the secret inherent in the "buried stone," Poem XII, using parallel figures ("seed" = "pit," "stone," and "tree"), expresses the inherent quality of life in all things which, unobserved, goes on quietly creating. The fate of future generations is not sealed in the stone (seed) but, rather, the promise of future generations is contained there, for the seed, lost by the bird

> will harbor in its branches most remote
> Descendants of the bird; while everywhere
> And unobserved, the soft green stalks and tubes
> Of water are hardening into wood, whose hide,
> Gnarled, knotted, flowing, and its hidden grain,
> Remember how the water is streaming still.

Here is the natural way, the water streaming in the hidden grain as opposed to the blood that streamed in Adam's tainted seed. This tree is a tree of life and is described by a poet who knows how trees grow and are nourished. What a lyrical and scientifically pleasing picture of a tree's annual growth, with the expansion and continuity of past, present, and future: the grain of seed becomes the grain of the tree, the "soft green stalks and tubes of water" harden into the "knotted, flowing" hide, as the generative force of water and seed work hidden mysteries within the tree.

The seed, as the subsequent lines state, is not the dry stone of IV, but is "asleep, as in a dream" where time (future and past) "is compacted under pressures of / Another order" and cracks open like a stone. But this stone does not shed blood (as in IV). It issues forth a stream that is something between "the raindrop and the sea"—the stream of life—which partakes of the raindrop (the melting moment) and the sea of eternity and runs always downward on its course (as it must, in time), gathering

> That bitter salt which spices us the food
> We sweat for, and the blood and tears we shed.

In the continuity of that stream, as we have seen before, all paradoxes merge. We spice our food with salt which we work for with the salty sweat of our brow. Our blood and tears pour into the stream. It is in *this* stream, ever flowing away, that the reality of man is written.[13]

RUNES, XIII

Poem XIII is both a continuation and a commentary on the mercantile, acquisitive theme of III, but it has a more cosmic setting. The vision is Joseph Conrad's, as expressed in *Heart of Darkness*[14] (which Nemerov quotes): "What greatness had not floated on the ebb of that river into the

13. Enjambment creates a sense of movement and vigor. The placement of "bird" (line 1), "branches" (line 2), and "bird" (line 3), all equidistant and having the *b* reiterated, strengthens the vital continuity between generations and stresses the symbiotic relationship between bird and tree. The repetition of *s* in line 4 ("soft," "stalks," "tubes") suggests the quiet secrecy of growth. In contrast, hard vowels and strong consonants in lines 5–6 (*w*, *n*, and *r*) emphasize the hardening cortex of the tree. In lines 7, 8, 11, and 12, the *s* and *ee* sounds, plus other soft vowels, simulate the sound of running water, in contrast to the hard rock (lines 8–9) which is suggested by strong syllables, having long vowels and sharp consonants, and assonance ("compacted"-"crack"). The alliterated *r* ("pressures," "order," "crack") is used in words which connote "breaking" or "force."

14. Conrad, p. 29. In "Runes," XIII, the swell of the sea and the roll of the ship are particularly well conveyed in the first ten lines. The parallel phrasing and repetition of "darkness" in line 5 emphasize the rise and fall of the waves, as well as mutability and the mystery of past and future. The sea is felt strongly again in lines 10–15. "Taste" (repeated twice), "lick," "saline," "cold," and the alliterated *l* enhance the very act of "licking" and the taste of salt.

mystery of an unknown earth! . . . The dreams of men, the seeds of commonwealths, the germs of empires." In Conrad's novel, Marlow penetrates the continental darkness of Africa, where he meets Kurtz and hears his dying words which tell of the dark desires of a lifetime. Marlow concludes that Kurtz is a remarkable man: "He had something to say. He said it. Since I peeped over the edge myself, I understood better the meaning of his stare, that could not see the flame of the candle, but was wide enough to embrace the whole universe, piercing enough to penetrate all the hearts that beat in the darkness."

In XIII, the dark sea of eternity is an "immense mirror" (reflecting man's shadow soul) where all rivers end, carrying with them "the dreams of men, the seeds of commonwealths, / The germs of Empire" (lines 1–3). Here the seed is extended from traders and sunflowers to nations and gains a paradoxical meaning: when used with "commonwealth," seed is a creative force but, when used with empire, it becomes the insidious germ. The national power that grows to an empire falls from overexpansion because of its lust for economic and political domination. This image parallels that of the sunflowers and traders (III) which also fell under their own weight. In the natural process and in man's political history, the poet sees the same pattern of growth, peak of power, and decline.

The mysterious sea goes to the ends of the earth and is a "many-veined bloodstream," swaying "the hulls / Of darkness gone, of darkness still to come . . ." (lines 3, 4, 5). As the swayer of hulls, the ocean is a destructive force, but it is also generative, for it sends "its tendrils steeping through the roots / Of wasted continents." Ocean recreates life on land from the ruins and waste of old life poured into her. The rhythm of time and the mystery of time eternal lie in the ocean;

. . . That echoing pulse
Carried the ground swell of all sea-returns

Muttering under history, and its taste,
Saline and cold, was as a mirror of
The taste of human blood. . . .

(lines 7–11)

The parallel of salt sea and bloodstream has been drawn before by Nemerov. Here, in the paradoxical generative-destructive might of the ocean, the sailor sees mirrored the destructive/creative nature of man, personified in the story of Cain and Abel. In licking the mirror clean, the sailor sees the other self, "the sacred Cain of blood / Who would seed a commonwealth in the Land of Nod." The reality is that of ocean, the destroyer and preserver of all. Man, like Cain,[15] would destroy and rebuild, but his destiny and dreams are impermanent; there is no Land of Nod, but only death. Nevertheless, the poem implies faith—not in man or his works, but in the great rhythm of the universe, in the dark mystery of ocean which continually creates form out of substance.

RUNES, XIV

In XIV, the two Ulysses figures of the second poem (two modes of life) are updated and internalized through the

15. Cain, in this context, suggests Leggatt in Conrad's *The Secret Sharer*. In an essay, "Composition and Fate in the Short Novel" (*PF*, 237), Nemerov has this to say about Conrad's story: "The young captain, irresolute and uncertain in his first command, comes face to face with his double: 'It was, in the night, as though I had been faced by my own reflection in the depths of a somber and immense mirror.' By protecting Leggatt (a legate from the darkness of the sea outside and the self within), by sharing his identity, by experiencing in homeopathic amounts the criminal element in his own nature, by at last liberating, or separating, this other self from his own at the risk of ship wreck, the young man gains a 'perfect communion' with his first command." In the following paragraph of the essay, Nemerov says this about Kurtz (*Heart of Darkness*), which further illumines "Runes," XIII: "So Kurtz is an instance of absolute power corrupted absolutely, yes, but this power is further characterized as that of the impulsive, archaic life liberated, which no man can bear and live, which Marlow himself nearly died of the briefest and most homeopathic contact with, and which in some sense is the force that makes history and makes civilization."

combined reflexive images of eye, water, and camera. The
first two images are parallel, with inverse meanings, and
demonstrate two ways of the mind in respect to the world.
The third image resolves the first two and defines imagination, with its possibilities and limitations, as a means of
relating mind and world. The heroic but doomed pursuit of
knowledge and virtue, which Dante's Ulysses undertook, is
suggested by the first image—that of the "strider" who
dares to walk on "drowning waters" (II, line 14).

> There is a threshold, that meniscus where
> The strider walks on drowning waters. . . .

The less daring path of compromise—the way taken by
Homer's Ulysses—underlies the second image, that of the
camera:

> . . . That tense, curved membrane of the camera's lens
> Which darkness holds against the battering light
> And the distracted drumming of the world's
> Importunate plenty. . . .

The camera probes only the surface of things, imitating
life but not grasping its substance. The photographer is
seen as barricading himself (within the small black box)
against the blinding light of reality and the rhythm of life
with its ups and downs. Not daring to actually experience
life, the photographer adjusts the world to himself (through
the camera's lens)—and himself to the world. (In the
camera, the person working the instrument adjusts the lens
to the light and darkness. In the human eye, the adjustment
of the lens is initiated by the light itself.) On the other
hand, the strider, wearing seven-league boots, dares to experience the dangerous tides of fortune and to seek the
light.

   The complexity of these images is clarified by Sher-

rington's passage on the eye, cited in Chapter 1. These
images represent two types of eyes (human and camera)
and have the dual connotation of "eye" and "mind"—or
perception and thought, combined in the term "mind's eye."
Both images are objective (in terms of image perceived)
and subjective (in terms of manner of perception). Nemerov makes the most of scientific terminology in his multivalent images and words. "Meniscus" is a crescent, referring to the undulation of the waves and of the lens of the
eye as it focuses on objects at varying distances. (The lens
of the eye is crystalline in appearance and is made up of
an outer layer of epithelial cells which envelop an elastic
protein capsule containing a clear, viscous fluid. In contrast
is the rigid curved camera lens.) "Threshold" signifies a
door, something that opens and shuts, and is associated
with all three images—water (waves), eye, and camera
lens. However, the watery threshold of waves and eye (line
1) contrasts to the dry, painless threshold of the camera's
lens (lines 3–4). "Threshold of pain" comes to mind and is
a valid connection, for it suggests human limits. (The tear-
water of the eye protects the anterior parts of the eye,
which are sensitive to pain.) The third image of the poem,
that of imagination, synthesizes the other two; it is mind
perceiving and mind creating. Both alternatives (in lines
1–6)—one impossible and the other undesirable—are combined in the way of imagination, as the agent of reality.
Recognizing that reality is perceived through reflexion, the
poet can only create reality through art which is temporal
yet contains something of the unfathomable mystery of the
eternal sea of darkness. "Threshold" becomes the "eye of
the mind" (imagination) "where the world walks / Deli-
cately. . . ." "Threshold of pain" (as part of the creative
process) is resolved in the needle image, for imagination is
"a needle threaded / From the reel of a raveling stream, to
stitch / Dissolving figures in a watered cloth. . . ." The
stream is the running, mutable light and dark water of life

from which the "damask either-sided" (shroud) of the lord
of Ithaca is made. Life is ultimately mysterious, yet the
shuttle of time ("the spidery oars") carries the ship (of
life) "To harbor in unfathomable mercies." The complex
image of Penelope, as Muse and Fate (weaving the damask
shroud by day, undoing her work at night) is drawn into
the needle image which pertains to art and imagination in
one of the loveliest passages Nemerov has written:[16]

> . . . Now that threshold,
> The water of the eye where the world walks
> Delicately, is as a needle threaded
> from the reel of a raveling stream, to stitch
> Dissolving figures in a watered cloth,
> A damask either-sided as the shroud
> Of the lord of Ithaca, labored at in light,
> Destroyed in darkness, while the spidery oars
> Carry his keel across deep mysteries
> To harbor in unfathomable mercies.

16. The rhythmical and musical devices in this poem are subtle,
for the poet's visual and audial imagination are expertly blended.
Enjambment is used, but stress is achieved by the fact that parallel
images are expressed in parallel phrases, enhanced by alliteration
and variance of beat. Heaviness is created through alliteration in
the following lines, suggesting the pull of the undertow: "The strider
walks on drowning waters . . ." (w, o, and a). At the same time we
have the impression of a giant of a man walking those waves. The
sound of the drum is caught in the alliterated d and in the rhythm of
the following lines: ". . . Which darkness holds against the battering
light / And the distracted drumming of the world's / Importunate
plenty." The repeated w and even beat of line 7 is broken by "Deli-
cately" (beginning line 8), which forces the reader to enunciate that
important word. Fluidity is expressed in lines 7–10 in the alliterated
r, l, s, and d. These lines are broken only by the word "stitch," which
pierces them like a needle. Contrast and emphasis are heightened by
alliteration in the following parallel phrases which simulate the movement of a shuttle (that of fate and time, and of Penelope) going back
and forth: "labored in light, / Destroyed in darkness. . . ." The
slant rhyme in the last two lines, "mysteries"-"mercies," makes death a
benign and gentle happening.

RUNES, XV

Man's separation from his source (the separation of mind/
body, mind/world), brought about by reflexivity, is resolved in XV, which gathers together all of the paradoxical
strands of the poem sequence into the full moment of being. Water and light are strong elemental images in this
poem. The poet becomes one with the secret of running
water and holds inside himself the secret seed—"the death-
less thing / Which it is death to open." Reflexivity bends
before the unfathomable mystery of being, for the poet
accepts what he knows and what he cannot know—the
strange process of life and death through which nature is
constantly renewed, that spiritual moment when one becomes part of all and is reborn through the death of consciousness of self. This is an April poem, a celebration of
life and the return of innocence and joy. One senses that
this is by no means a permanent state of being, for the
dark moods, the going under and rising, will happen again.
Nevertheless, in moving between thought and thing, the
poet, through imagination, finds the world revealed to him
as in a glass darkly and can, finally, merge into the deeper
reality he can never know.[17]

Although "Runes" was first published in *Poetry* in
February of 1959, it remains the finest expression of Nemerov's thought and genius and contains the "philosophy
of minimal affirmation," which is more fully elucidated in
his subsequent poems. In "Runes" the poet returns to the
source of "great primary human drama", thereby returning to the mystery of Creation, wherein lie the secret beginnings of art. Through imagination, as the agent of
reality, the poet reveals the divine shadow of nature's
signature on all things. "Runes" brings back to us "the sub-

17. Secrecy and quiet are expressed in the narrative epigram
and through alliteration in the first line ("To watch water, to watch
running water. . . ."). The movement of water is felt in the following

lime and terrible treasure that was lost," now transformed
into something rich and strange, for the poem is a continuous revelation of "articulating possibilities still unknown" in a universe where "things must be continuous
with themselves, / As with whole worlds that they themselves are not, / In order that they may be so transformed."

---

lines through the tripping syllables and the repeated *l*, *r*, *s*, and *c*.
A crescendo occurs in lines 11–13 and one feels the ebb and flow of
the tide of the eternal sea. The poem sequence ends quietly and
secretly as it began, for the Mystery remains.

5

A GREAT RECKONING
IN A LITTLE ROOM

THROUGH HIS POEMS and his concept of imagination as the agent of reality, Nemerov has envisioned a faith based on affirmation through doubt. This faith, as well as its articulation, derives in many ways from that of his fore-fathers and cannot be construed as dogma, since the Old Testament bred prophets, not theologians. In his idea of poetry as a doctrine of signatures, in his reflexive turn of mind and proclivity to doubt, and in his refusal to utter the ineffable name of Y-H-W-H, Nemerov is true to his Jewish heritage. Any attempt to limit God by naming Him, or to circumscribe the Mystery with a religious system, is tanta-mount to idolatry, for He is the One Who answered Moses: "I AM THAT I AM."[1] Yet the poet feels and sees the Divine Presence in the world and responds to It directly as did the psalmist—whether in imprecatory songs or in hymns of praise. The first two commandments of the Law are the basis of much of Nemerov's thought, particularly in his rejection of earthen images and all forms of idolatry and artifice which separate man from his source.

The prophetic voice can be heard in Nemerov's poems,

1. Exodus 3:14. In the Torah, the translation is "I WILL BE THAT I WILL BE."

in his essays about poetry, and in his attitude toward his work. The model of the creative process is the first chapter of Genesis, where God creates and names the world. Poetry is a continual revelation of the Word, although the poet is aware that the Word Itself is unspeakable and that the "moment of expressiveness" is only an echo, or a shadow of truth. The poet says that "this moment of expressiveness itself occurs at a crossing point, and tells us that something in language is not linguistic, that something in reason is not reasonable. It speaks of a relation between inside and outside, an identity between inside and outside, but this relation, this identity, is itself unspeakable. . . ." The poet adds that "we might say of expressiveness itself, of the irreducible phrase, that first it is, and then it finds a meaning in the world."[2]

Expressiveness finds a meaning in the world through imagination. By echoing what is not linguistic in language and by reflecting what is not reasonable in reason, imagination affirms the unspeakable and the invisible in the mirror of language. Though both aural and visual aspects of imagination are related in Nemerov's work, the primary function of imagination is aural. In "The Swaying Form" the poet tells us that "a poem, whether of two lines or ten thousand, is therefore the name of something, and in its ideal realm of fiction or illusion it corresponds to what is said of the Divine Name in several significant respects:

It is unique.
It can never be repeated.
It brings into being the situation it names, and is therefore truly a creation.
It is secret, even while being perfectly open and public, for it defines a thing which could not have been known without it" (*PF*, 14).

2. "Bottom's Dream: The Likeness of Poems and Jokes," pp. 555–56.

A similar thought is stated in the poem "The Painter Dreaming in the Scholar's House," which relates the aural and visual qualities of imagination:

> . . . It is because
> Language first rises from the speechless world
> That the painterly intelligence
> Can say correctly that he makes his world,
> Not imitates the one before his eyes.
>
> (I, lines 17–21)

And later in the poem the same idea is expressed conversely:

> . . . Only because the world
> Already is a language can the painter speak
> According to the grammar of the ground.
>
> It is archaic speech, that has not yet
> Divided up its cadences in words;
> It is a language for the oldest spells
> About how some thoughts rose into the mind
> While others, stranger still, sleep in the world.
>
> (II, lines 18–25)

Nemerov's concepts of imagination as dominantly aural and of nature as responsive to language are borne out in his vision of a universe which, "so far as we relate ourselves to it by the mind, may be not so much a meaning as a rhythm, a continuous articulation of question and answer, question and answer, a musical dialectic precipitating out moments of meaning which become distinct only as one wave does in a sea of waves." This musical dialectic, the natural model for which is sea and stream, is articulated and ritualized in the poem and in the poetic process. In all respects, poetry is a ritual for Nemerov—"a spiritual exercise," or "attempt to pray one's humanity back into the universe; and conversely an attempt to read, to derive anew, one's humanity from nature, nature considered as a book, a dictionary and bible at once." Poetry, like prayer, always reaches its beginning again, because of the essential quality of relation which endures in form itself. This likeness between the two types of ritual can be clarified by a passage from Martin Buber's *I and Thou,* which describes form itself and parallels much of what Nemerov has to say about poetry: "Form is also a mixture of Thou and It. In belief and in a cult form can harden into an object; but, in virtue of the essential quality of relation that lives on in it, it continually becomes present again. God is near His forms so long as man does not remove them from Him. In true prayer belief and cult are united and purified to enter into the living relation."[3]

The poem as ritual and the poet's reflexive, aural imagination, with its emphasis on the verb, stem from Hebrew tradition. The Hebrew imagination, rooted in a direct I-Thou relationship, was often expressed in reflexive verbs (including the verb meaning "to pray") and was strongly aural. Psalms, as part of religious ritual, were originally chanted, and the ancient music can still be heard in their great rolling phrases and powerful rhythms. Much of Nemerov's most vivid aural and visual imagery is drawn from the Old Testament and, sometimes, from the Gospels.

Yet the poet's intelligence is many-faceted, displaying other strands of his Western heritage and revealing a scholarly understanding of the classics, Greek mythology, philosophy, science, and the arts. His visual imagination, his eye for paradox and antitheses, and his dedication to the demands of form, derive from the classical Greek imagination, which, unlike the Hebrew, found its noblest expression in architecture, the plastic arts, drama, and philosophy. Highly abstract and intellectual, the Greek mind was both unitive and diverse in focus. This duality, so apparent in

3. Page 118.

the philosophical and scientific dialogue of the Golden Age, was articulated in terms of the one versus the many, the absolute versus the relative, the universal versus the particular, the eternal versus the temporal, and the ideal versus the actual—dualisms which have since been merged in the Apollonian-Dionysian antinomy. In much of Nemerov's work this antinomy is evident: in his double vision, in his use of tragicomic paradox, and in the two dominant strains of the poet's voice.

However, in the arts the unitive aspect of the Greek mind prevailed, through its emphasis on form, and it is this aspect of the classical legacy that Nemerov both accepts and rejects. During the Hellenic period (and well into the Hellenistic), balance, proportion, and harmony were the criteria by which an art work was judged—especially in architecture and sculpture, where the ideal became an end in itself. In creating formal and spatial relationships, the sculptor, no less than the architect, relied on numerical ratios and mathematical principles, as well as on his daemon. Through perfection of form, the sculptor sought to express a universal ideal, which to the Greeks was far more "real" than a literal or individualized representation. This ideal (a Platonic concept) was that which could be summarized in the nouns: beauty, truth, wisdom, virtue, love, etc. Although Nemerov rejects the idealistic thrust of classicism— as he also rejects statues and monuments and "nouns of stone"—he still regards form as existential evidence of a deeper reality. In art, as in nature, form is an extension of (and, therefore, essential to) the creative process—not as an end in itself, but as the means through which revelation occurs.

Because of his versatility in style, his range in tone, and the complexity of his vision and imagination, Nemerov's achievements as a poet and essayist defy summary and, as a whole, are beyond the scope of this work. Subsequent studies may profitably explore his humor and wit (which run the gambit from sophisticated satire and tragi-comic paradox to sheer buffoonery) or his deft use of scientific imagery, most clearly exemplified in "The First Day" (*BS*); both of these subjects have only been touched upon here. Some of his best poems are the dramatic monologues: "Mrs. Mandrill," "Death and the Maiden," "The Vacuum," and "Zalmoxis" (*NSP*); "At a Country Hotel," "Lot Later," and "The Private Eye" (*NRD*); and, perhaps, the most intriguing and difficult of all, "The Beekeeper Speaks . . . and is Silent" (*BS*). All of these poems merit study, as do the two plays *Endor* and *Cain* and the thirty-seven essays in *Poetry & Fiction*, only a few of which are cited in this study. As an essayist, Nemerov's style is distinct, witty, and provocative. His insights are always original, however worn his subject, and he discusses a variety of topics with perspicuity and flair.

This particular exploration, which focuses primarily on the poet's use of elemental imagery in the initiatory ascent, can serve only as an introduction to Nemerov's poems and essays. Nevertheless, some of what has been discovered is generally applicable to Nemerov's work. First of all, poetry, or writing, is a way of being, as he continually tells us: "Writing is a species of 'askesis,' a persevering devotion to the energy passing between self and world. It is a way of living, a way of being, and, though it does produce results in the form of 'works,' these may come to seem of secondary importance to the person so engaged." The poet adds, with characteristic humor, that this species of askesis works within "an ideal or fictional, rather than a practical realm, so it purifies not the character but the style."[4]

Nemerov's most consistent stance over the years, despite his sensitive ear and aural imagination, has been as commentator on the action, rather than as lyricist. His particular talent and temperament, combined with his early set of experiences, do not enable him to take off his vest and

4. "The Swaying Form," in *PF*, p. 14.

sing in the manner of Robert Burns or Dylan Thomas. Because of his intellect, wit, and reserve, Nemerov is a master of the long philosophical poem, the ironical portrait, and the incisive epigram. He says of himself: "Perhaps that situation, in which through no fault of my own but through the physiological process of growing up I had to abandon the heroic roles for those of the villain, counselor, commentator on the action, and maybe buffoon, formed the early model for the position I most often take with respect to writing, favoring an ironic clarity and a depth of tone to the unreserved lyric bursting forth" (*Journal*, 79).

Nevertheless, the pervasive quality is lyrical, even in the philosophical poems, because the poet, however much he is the commentator, is a musician also with a humble, implicit faith in a deeper reality. Perhaps his most significant development, from his early to his later poems, is the dialectic between poet and world, moving toward a wholeness of vision which is never static. This development, following the ascent pattern in terms of elemental imagery, may have evolved from the poet's deepening response to the natural world and to nature as the source of language. A possible corollary to this development is the poet's growing tendency to simplify his style by cutting away all that is irrelevant, obscure, or superimposed, in order to "say over the certain simplicities, / The running water and the standing stone. . . ." In referring to this tendency among poets, Nemerov states: "With all the reverence poets have for tradition, poetry is always capable of reaching its beginning again. Its tradition, ideally, has to do with reaching the beginning, so that, of many young poets who begin with literature, a few old ones may end up with nature" ("Younger Poets: The Lyric Difficulty," in *PF*, 224).

Although elemental imagery and the ascent pattern are part of poetic tradition, Nemerov's poetic vocabulary and idiom, evolving from earth, water, space, and light, are original. So is his unique development of the reflexive image and the narrative epigram, which are excellent techniques to convey his prismatic vision and aural imagination. Water and light are dominant elements in his work. Together they are the generative force of creation, identified with body and mind, respectively. The dark unfathomable sea, the shadow of eternity, is the mother of all being. Man carries the salt sea in his blood. Our human span is a stream—between the momentary raindrop and the endless sea. In the stream is the rhythm of life which pulses to the vast oceanic rhythm of eternity. Through light, mind imagines the world and sees its own image reflected there. Through the light of imagination man relates to the invisible deep—in the world beyond him and in the dark abyss of his own being.

The poet's preoccupation with light imagery in his later work grows out of a concern for spiritual matters and for the problem of mind in relation to world—the problem of imagination. Although Nemerov never loses his sense of the ironic or his doubting attitude, a quiet faith illumines most of these poems, even when the poet is acting as commentator on the scene. In his search for meaning and a simpler, purer mode of expression the poet is following, in his own way, the road taken by Frost, where the natural signs are riddles and epigrams. In October 1970 Nemerov wrote: "In my old age I'm turning more to the runic and riddling, and in fact tend to see riddles as the very basis of poetry; must presently write something about that, too. Wonderful the way a single thought turns imperialist and wants to take over a whole world: as soon as I thought of riddles as the model I was able to see that the dictionary is composed of nothing but riddles, concealed from us by the circumstance that the answer is always given before the question."[5]

In the December 1970 issue of *Poetry* a group of Nemerov's epigrams and riddles appeared.[6] (All but three of

5. Personal letter, October 18, 1970.
6. Pages 149–53. "Being of Three Minds," "Embarrassment

these will be included in Nemerov's eighth volume of poetry, *Gnomes and Occasions,* tentatively scheduled for fall 1972 publication.) Three of the poems are satiric epigrams: "Embarrassment Lives! on TV, Anyhow," "Item," and "Behavior." The ironic twist and satirical thrust in these poems is razor-sharp and pointed at the hypocrisies and absurd pretensions of our society. The wittiest of these epigrams is "Item," which specifically plays upon the absurdities of scientific thought and planning in relation to the field of geriatrics and is a cool indictment of our callous treatment of the aged.

I heard this morning on the news
They plan to colonize the moon
With senior citizens (or olds)

The less the pull of gravity
(the scientific theory goes)
The less the strain upon the heart

One adds: the less the atmosphere
(We know the moon has none at all)
The less the strain upon the nose

His other epigrams as well as his riddles are more philosophical in tone, although they are also "witty" in the eighteenth-century meaning of that word. The couplet (an eighteenth-century device) appears frequently in these poems, which are tightly structured in both rhyme and meter, so that a number of complex thoughts and attitudes are expressed with the greatest economy of style. Often a whimsical note comes through, and the riddles, like their Anglo-Saxon prototype, have an aura of magic or mystery about them. These poems are fun to read, though one cannot be sure to what extent the poet is playing games with

---

Lives! on TV, Anyhow," "Solipcism & Solecism," "Item," "Prism," "Behavior," "Quaerendo Invenietis."

his readers. However, the element of play is part of poetry, especially of riddles, as Nemerov explains in his essay "Bottom's Dream: The Likeness of Poems and Jokes."

These riddles and epigrams either center on or depart from the problem of imagination (the relation of mind to world) or speak of the phenomena of vision and language in terms of the creative process. The following quatrain, "Solipcism & Solecism," is an epigrammatic statement about the paradox of vision and two ways of the mind:

> Strange about shadows, but the sun
> Has never seen a single one.
> Should night be mentioned by the moon
> He'd be appalled at what he's done.

The ironic view in this quatrain is more emphatic in "Being of Three Minds," which derides, somewhat sardonically, the polar extremes of reason and faith, logic and passion (or appetite), etc. While the antinomy (which is, in a sense, Apollonian-Dionysian) is not resolved in the concluding heroic couplet, the problem of mind perceiving is suggested:

> Some spellers say it was the little i
> That differences deify and defy.

"Prism" is about the nature of vision, and about language as a mirror of nature, through which a transference occurs and a relationship between thought and thing is effected.

> It corners the sun and caroms one
> Rainbow to either side, an un-
> Assuming virtuoso. True
> That both the cue ball and the cue
> Shatter on impact, but they yield
> The spectrum of objects, the green field.

Perhaps the most intriguing of the poems is "Quaerendo Invenietis"—the concluding inscription of this study—which consists of three riddles that form a statement about language and communication. Each of these riddles, like any true riddle, has a specific answer which the reader will recognize when he discovers it. Yet, like any good poem, "Quaerendo Invenietis" can be interpreted in various interesting ways and survive them all.

The group of epigrams and riddles in *Poetry* and a recent poem, "The Tapestry,"[7] indicate clearly the direction in which Nemerov is moving—toward a simpler, more immediate and economical mode of expression. The ideas and intentions of his later poems, as a whole, are no less complex than in his earlier ones, but the poet's vision has become more unitive; it implies a faith that is too mysterious to talk about but involves the element of play and a feeling that poetry is an act of faith—a way of being and becoming, a way of prayer. In his later poems Nemerov shows us more facets of the primary human drama. The poet of the

---

7. In *Michigan Quarterly* 10, no. 3 (Summer 1971): 187. The poem was sent to me by Nemerov as a possible "colophon" for this book. It is a very good poem but, for many reasons, "Quaerendo Invenietis" seems a more appropriate ending.

The Tapestry

On this side of the tapestry
There sits the bearded king,
And round about him stand
His lords and ladies in a ring.
His hunting dogs are there,
And armed men at command.

On that side of the tapestry
The formal court is gone,
The kingdom is unknown;
Nothing but thread to see,
Knotted and rooted thread
Spelling a world unsaid.

Men do not find their ways
Through a seamless maze,
And all direction lose
In a labyrinth of clues,
A forest of loose ends
Where sewing never mends.

early poems was sometimes "offish." Even when satirizing Eliot's use of allusion, Nemerov is still identifying with Eliot, or perhaps is in the process of breaking that identification.[8] In his more recent poems (1963 through 1971) Nemerov has reached that stage of the journey where he takes the reader with him, into his own ambit, by becoming one with him.

Nemerov's imagination remains complex, but the reflexive image stands forth now with greater clarity, as we see in "Prism" and in "Quaerendo Invenietis," despite the deliberate ambiguity of the riddle. The tragicomic paradox has been refined and sharpened to become a more delicate and piercing tool—a needle rather than a dagger. The poet has mastered that most difficult of skills, the art of communicating through what is *not* said. A single epigram conveys a world of meaning.

Throughout Nemerov's work is the awareness of an Eternal Mystery which is accessible only as it is reflected in the mirror of language. The mirror is shatterproof, as far as man is concerned, for he cannot break it through the power of mind imagining, nor can he look beyond. Yet, through language, first, is the world made comprehensible and the divine shadow perceived. In recognizing this situation—with all of its inherent risks, perils, limitations, and possibilities—the "predecessor of Perseus" has faced the unbearable She of the world in the mirror of his shield and, by naming, has subdued her. To name is to create something out of darkness and doubt, and what the mind invents it also discovers. Vision is the life substance of a poem; "but the road goes on." Through his poetry and through the act of writing, Nemerov affirms the truth of his own words: "And it is thus that art, by vision and not by dogma, patiently and repeatedly offers the substance of things hoped for, the evidence of things unseen."[9]

8. "On the Threshold of His Greatness, the Poet Comes Down with a Sore Throat," in *NRD*, pp. 63–65.
9. "The Swaying Form," in *PF*, p. 16.

Quaerendo Invenietis

I

I am the combination to a door
That fools and wise with equal ease undo.
Your unthought thoughts are changes still unread
In me, without whom nothing's to be said.

II

Without my meaning nothing, nothing means.
I am the wave for which the worlds make way.
A term of time, and sometimes too of death,
I am the silence in the things you say.

III

It is a spiral way that trues my arc
Toward central silence and my unreached mark.
Singing and saying till his time be done,
The traveler does nothing. But the road goes on.

NOTE: It would be most unfair not to divulge the answers to the riddles, especially since Nemerov has done so in recent lectures. Therefore, the answers are given at the end of this footnote, where they may be read by those who wish to know them, or covered up and bypassed by the more adventurous souls who like to solve riddles. If you are of the second type, you may find a clue in Nemerov's concept of the universe being not so much a meaning as a rhythm (a kind of "musical dialectic," insofar as we relate to it by mind), or in his ideas that nature is a dictionary and poetry is a doctrine of signatures. Another clue is that a separate (though not dissimilar) geometric pattern exists in each riddle; for example, III is given in lines and circularities. But, perhaps the best solution is to take each riddle, singly, and ponder the meanings of each word in its context.

At present, I have a large portfolio of interesting, possible answers which have been obtained from a number of professors at Lake Forest College, from literary friends, and from my freshman and junior students, last spring, at New Trier East High School. (The librarian at the school was both amazed and delighted at the sudden influx of students looking for the December 1970 issue of *Poetry*!) Very few people whom I have approached have found the answers. Some people have guessed one, and others, two; no one, as far as I know, has guessed all three. However, the various interpretations are too intriguing to dismiss; they will be discussed in an essay on the poem.

The answers to "Quaerendo Invenietis" are: I, the alphabet; II, a sentence; III, the tone arm moving across the record.

SELECT BIBLIOGRAPHY

Works of Howard Nemerov

POETRY

The Image and the Law. New York: Henry Holt, 1947.
Guide to the Ruins. New York: Random House, 1950.
The Salt Garden. Boston: Little, Brown and Co., 1955.
Mirrors & Windows: Poems. Chicago: University of Chicago Press, 1958.
New & Selected Poems. Chicago: University of Chicago Press, 1960.
The Next Room of the Dream. Chicago: University of Chicago Press, 1962.
The Blue Swallows. Chicago: University of Chicago Press, 1967.
The Painter Dreaming in the Scholar's House, to the Memory of the Painters, Paul Klee and Paul Terrence Feeley. New York: The Phoenix Book Shop, 1968. (Inaugural poem composed for and delivered at the Inauguration of the President of Boston College, the Very Reverend W. Seavey Joyce, S.J., October 20, 1968, at the McHugh Forum, Boston College, Chestnut Hill, Massachusetts.)
"Being of Three Minds," "Embarrassment Lives! on TV, Anyhow," "Solipcism & Solecism," "Item," "Prism," "Behavior," "Quaerendo Invenietis," *Poetry* 117, no. 3 (December 1970): 149–53.
"The Tapestry," *Michigan Quarterly* 10, no. 3 (Summer 1971): 187.

CURRENT AMERICAN REPRINTS

The Next Room of the Dream. Chicago: University of Chicago Press, Phoenix Books, 1965.
New & Selected Poems. Chicago: University of Chicago Press, Phoenix Books, 1967.

MISCELLANEOUS UNPUBLISHED MATERIAL

Personal letter, June 23, 1968.
Personal letter, October 9, 1968.
Personal letter, October 30, 1968.
Personal letter, June 22, 1969.
Personal letter, October 18, 1970.
Personal letter, September 27, 1971.

PROSE, CRITICAL ESSAYS, AND LECTURES

Poetry and Fiction: Essays. New Brunswick, N.J.: Rutgers University Press, 1963.
Journal of the Fictive Life. New Brunswick, N.J.: Rutgers University Press, 1965.
"Attentiveness and Obedience." In *Poets on Poetry,* edited by Howard Nemerov. New York: Basic Books, 1966.
"Bottom's Dream: The Likeness of Poems and Jokes." *Virginia Quarterly Review,* no. 43 (Autumn 1966). (This was Nemerov's first lecture as consultant to the Library of Congress, delivered on October 7, 1963). Reprint.
"The Mind's Relation with the World, Two Ways of the Imagination." *Graduate Journal* 7, no. 2 (Spring 1967): 375–97.
"Speculative Equations; Poems, Poets, Computers." *The American Scholar,* Summer 1967, pp. 394–414.
Reflexions on Poetry & Poetics. New Brunswick, N.J.: Rutgers University Press, 1972.

CRITICAL ARTICLES, ESSAYS, AND REVIEWS
ON HOWARD NEMEROV'S POEMS

Bogan, Louise. "Books, Verse." *New Yorker,* April 1, 1961, pp. 129–31.
Burke, Kenneth. "Comments on Eighteen Poems by Howard Nemerov." *Sewanee Review* 60 (1952): 117–31.
Dickey, James. *Babel to Byzantium, Poets and Poetry Now.* Pp. 35–41. New York: Farrar, Strauss, and Giroux, 1968.
Engle, Paul. "Books." *New York Herald Tribune,* July 30, 1961, p. 7.
Gunn, Thom. "Outside Faction." *Yale Review,* n.s. 50 (June 1961): 585.
Harvey, Robert D. "A Prophet Armed: An Introduction to the Poetry of Howard Nemerov." In *Poets in Progress,* edited by E. B. Hungerford, pp. 111–13. Evanston, Ill.: Northwestern University Press, 1962.
Jarrell, Randall. "Recent Poetry." *Yale Review,* no. 45 (September 1955): 122–32.
Kizer, Carolyn. "Nemerov: The Middle of the Journey." *Poetry* 93, no. 3 (December 1958): 178–81.
Koch, Vivienne. "The Necessary Angels of Earth," *Sewanee Review* 59 (1951): 674–75.

Meinke, Peter. *Howard Nemerov.* Pamphlets on American Writers, no. 70. Minneapolis: University of Minnesota Press, 1968.

Rexroth, Kenneth. "A Stranger on Madison Avenue." *New York Times Book Review,* January 8, 1961, p. 53.

Whittemore, Reed. "Observations of an Alien." *New Republic* 138 (June 23, 1958): 27–28.

Williams, Miller. "Transaction with the Muse." *Saturday Review,* March 9, 1968, p. 32.

MISCELLANEOUS REFERENCE MATERIAL

Beevers, John. *St. Teresa of Ávila.* pp. 143–44. Garden City, N.Y.: Doubleday & Co., 1961.

Brooks, Cleanth. *The Well-Wrought Urn.* New York: Harcourt, Brace and World, 1947.

Buber, Martin. *I and Thou.* Trans. by Ronald Gregory Smith. New York: Charles Scribner's Sons, 1953.

Carson, Rachel L. *The Sea around Us.* New York: Oxford University Press, 1951.

Conrad, Joseph. *Heart of Darkness, Almayer's Folly, The Lagoon.* New York: Dell Publishing Co., 1960.

Eliot, Thomas Stearns. "The Sacred Wood." *Selected Essays.* 3rd ed. London: Faber and Faber, 1961.

Frazer, Sir James George. *The Golden Bough, A Study in Magic and Religion.* Abridged ed. New York: Macmillan Co., 1942.

Friesen, Otto von and Joshua Whatmough. *Encyclopaedia Britannica.* 14th ed., 1969 printing. S.v. "rune."

McLuhan, Marshall and Parker Harley. *Through the Vanishing Point: Space in Poetry and Painting.* New York: Harper & Row, 1968.

Milton, John. *The Complete Works.* Edited by Douglas Bush. Boston: Houghton Mifflin Co., 1965.

Ogden, C. K. and I. A. Richards. *The Meaning of Meaning, A Study of the Influence of Language upon Thought and of Science on Symbolism, with Supplementary Essays by B. Malinowski and F. G. Crookshank.* New York: Harcourt, Brace and Co., 1923.

Proust, Marcel. *Swann's Way,* vol. 1: *Remembrance of Things Past.* Trans. C. K. Scott Moncrieff. New York: Random House, 1934.

Ransom, John Crowe. "Poetry: A Note in Ontology." In *The World's Body,* pp. 111–42. New York: Charles Scribner's Sons, 1938.

Shakespeare, William. *The Complete Works.* Edited by G. B. Harrison, New York: Harcourt, Brace and World, 1952.

————. *Troilus and Cressida.* Edited by Harold N. Hildebrand. New Variorum ed. Philadelphia: J. B. Lippincott, 1953.

Waxman, Meyer, Rabbi. *Encyclopaedia Britannica.* 14th ed., 1969 printing. S.v. "Jewish Holidays."

Weston, Jessie L. *From Ritual to Romance.* New York: Doubleday & Co., 1957.

Whitehead, Alfred North. *Science and the Modern World.* New York: Macmillan Co., 1925.

INDEX